佛弟子常於晝夜至心誦念八大

一覺悟世間無常。國土危脆。四大

爲無主。心是惡源形爲罪藪如是

二覺知多欲爲苦生死疲勞從貪

三覺知心無厭足惟得多求增長

佛弟子常於晝夜、至心誦念八大

一覺悟、世間無常。國土危脆。四大

僞無主。心是惡源形爲罪藪如是

二覺知、多欲爲苦生死疲勞、從貪

三覺知、心無厭足惟得多求增長

BUDDHISM

pure and simple

Other books in English by Master Hsing Yun:

Being Good: Buddhist Ethics for Everyday Life

Only a Great Rain :A Guide to Chinese Buddhist Meditation

Lotus in a Stream: Essays in Basic Buddhism

Where Is Your Buddha Nature? Stories to Instruct and Inspire

Describing the Indescribable: A Commentary on the Diamond Sutra

Cloud and Water: An Interpretation of Ch'an Poems

Humble Table, Wise Fare: Hospitality for the Heart

BUDDHISM

pure and simple

A Commentary on the

Sutra of the Eight Realizations of Great Beings

by

MASTER HSING YUN

translated by Tom Graham

New York · **WEATHERHILL** · *Tokyo*

First edition, 2001

Published by Weatherhill, Inc.

41 Monroe Turnpike, Trumbull, Connecticut 06611

Printed in the United States.

Library of Congress Cataloging-in-Publication Data available on request.

CONTENTS

SUTRA OF THE

EIGHT REALIZATIONS

OF GREAT BEINGS

For all disciples of the Buddha:
morning and night,
hold them in your mind,
and chant them often,
these eight realizations
of great beings.

One: Realize that this world is impermanent, that nations are unsafe and unstable, that the four elements cause suffering and are empty, and that there is no self within the five skandhas; that all things that arise must change and decline, and that they are but false appearances without any stable essence; that the mind is the source of evil, and that form is a congregation of wrongdoings. Contemplate all of this, and gradually you will disentangle yourself from the cycle of birth and death.

Two: Realize that excessive desire causes suffering. The fatigue and troubles of the cycle of birth and death arise from greed and desire. Have few desires, be receptive, and you will be content in body and mind.

Three: Realize that the mind is insatiable, and that it constantly strives for more, thus adding to its transgressions and mistakes. The bodhisattva is not like this; he thinks often of being satisfied with what he has, and he is peaceful in poverty and upholds the Dharma. Wisdom is his only concern.

Four: Realize that laziness leads to downfall. Be diligent and break the hold of harmful fixations. Defeat the four demons and escape the prison of this dark world.

Five: Realize that ignorance gives rise to the cycle of birth and death. The bodhisattva studies widely, listens carefully, and thinks often in order to increase his wisdom and develop his talents in speaking so that he is fit to teach and transform others, and show them the greatest joy.

Six: Realize that resenting poverty and suffering leads only to more of the same. A bodhisattva is generous and equal minded toward both friend and foe. He does not dwell on old wrongs, or make new enemies.

Seven: Realize that the five desires bring nothing but trouble. Though we live in this world, we do not become stained by worldly pleasures. Instead, we think often of a monk's garb, his bowl, and his chanting instruments. Having set our minds on monastic life, we uphold the way and purify ourselves. Our morality encompasses all, our compassion includes everyone.

Eight: Realize that life and death are like flickering flames, and that suffering is endless. Take the Mahayana Vow to befriend all things. Vow to take on the illimitable sufferings of sentient beings, and to lead them all to ultimate bliss.

These eight points are the realizations of all Buddhas and bodhisattvas. With diligence they trod the way, with compassion *they hone their wisdom. They board the vessel of the Dharma body, and sail to the shore of nirvana. Then they return to the cycle of birth and death to help others cross to that shore. These eight points can direct us in all things, and they can show all sentient beings how to understand the sufferings of birth and death; they can help us disentangle ourselves from the five desires and turn our minds to the saintly way. If a disciple of the Buddha chants these eight points, thought by thought he will eradicate his infinite karmic debt; and he will approach the awakened state, and quickly become enlightened; then he will forever be free from the cycle of birth and death, and abide in joy forever.*

BUDDHISM

pure and simple

INTRODUCTION

An Overview of the Sutra

A BASIC TEACHING OF THE BUDDHA IS THAT ALL THINGS ARE CAUSED and that nothing comes into being without a reason. This way of thinking is so fundamental to Buddhism that all Buddhist sutras begin with an explanation of the causes that led to their inceptions. There is only one exception to this rule—the *Sutra of the Eight Realizations of Great Beings*. This sutra does not have an introductory section that tells where the sutra was spoken, to whom it was spoken, and who was responsible for remembering it. The introductory part of this sutra may have been left off when it was translated into Chinese near the end of the second century of the common era. It is possible that the teaching seemed more immediate and convincing to its translator without an introduction, especially since he knew of the great wealth of Buddhist literature that would soon follow it into China.

The *Sutra of the Eight Realizations of Great Beings* is one of the first Buddhist sutras ever translated into Chinese. It reads like a short summary of Mahayana Buddhism, and surely it was selected for early translation for precisely this reason. It is char-

13

acterized by its brevity, clarity, and completeness. Brevity should not be confused with shallowness. The *Sutra of the Eight Realizations of Great Beings* is a mature compendium of the main ideas of Mahayana Buddhism. Its early translation into Chinese was clearly an attempt to introduce Buddhism to an intelligent and receptive non-Buddhist Chinese audience. This sutra, along with the *Sutra in Forty-two Sections,* which is the first sutra translated into Chinese and is also a brief work, prepared China for the vast body of Buddhist literature that was to pour into it over the next five centuries.

The eight realizations discussed in this sutra are also mentioned in the *Agamas,* the *Sutra of Bequeathed Teachings,* and the *Treatise on the Completion of Truth.* The original Sanskrit version of the sutra has been lost.

Tradition has it that the teaching contained in the *Sutra of the Eight Realizations of Great Beings* was prompted by a question asked of the Buddha by one of his wisest disciples, Aniruddha. While the Buddha was staying at the Jeta Grove in Sravasti, Aniruddha is reported to have asked him the following question: "Oh Buddha, those of us who are monks know that our behavior must be guided by the Six Harmonies, and that we must be selfless with each other. We also know that we must treat all other sentient beings with compassion and kindness. Oh Buddha, how are people who are not monks to behave? And how are those of us who are monks to behave when we interact with lay people? Please tell us how lay people are to become enlightened and how they should behave if they want to achieve nirvana."

The Buddha replied, "Aniruddha, you have asked a good question. This question pertains to the realizations of all great beings. I will now explain to you that which, night and day, you should hold in your mind…"

The *Sutra of the Eight Realizations of Great Beings* has been praised by Buddhist masters down through the centuries. Its greatness lies in its emphasis on the importance of life in this world. Though it is a short text, it is infinitely valuable because it shows how the Buddha intended his teachings to be used. This sutra is like a compass and navigational chart. It offers all of the wisdom we will ever need to steer our lives away from confusion and fear toward the peace and security of the shores of truth.

THE TEACHER AND THE TEACHING

Shakyamuni Buddha, who is the speaker of this sutra, was born a prince in Kapilavastu, in what is now Nepal. At the age of twenty-nine, he renounced all of his worldly privileges to pursue the truth. After six years of ascetic practice, he became enlightened one evening while meditating under a bodhi tree. For the next forty-five years, he taught others how to realize what he had seen. The generosity and compassion that he displayed in teaching the Dharma for so many years form a living core around which all of the rest of Buddhism clusters. Shakyamuni Buddha's example stands as a constant reminder that the well being of others is fully as important as our own.

The word *Buddha* means "enlightened one" or "awakened one." Only a human being can become a Buddha. Shakyamuni Buddha is the Buddha of our realm. He is usually referred to as "the Buddha." There are many other Buddhas residing in many other realms in the universe. The Buddha taught that there are more Buddha realms in the universe than there are grains of sand in the Ganges River. Just as the night sky teems with stars, so the universe is teeming with life.

Shakyamuni Buddha did not invent the truths that he

taught. He discovered them. He taught that all human beings can do what he did. He said that when a human being makes his consciousness perfectly pure, he will see the truth that underlies all things. In that moment he will become enlightened. As we delve more deeply into the *Sutra of the Eight Realizations of Great Beings*, we will learn much more about the truths that the Buddha taught. His teachings are often described as a path because they lead us toward discovering the truth for ourselves. The truths of Buddhism are living truths and they cannot be handed to us by anyone. They must be discovered and experienced by each and every one of us. The purpose of the Dharma is to teach us how to see for ourselves.

The words *great beings* in the title of this sutra refer to enlightened beings—Buddhas and bodhisattvas. A Buddha is a fully enlightened being, while a bodhisattva is someone who has a measure of enlightenment. The enlightenment of a bodhisattva, though it is not as great as a Buddha, is sufficient to cause him or her to understand that all conscious beings are one and that to live within the truth means to live for the good of others.

The word *bodhisattva* is a compound of two Sanskrit words *bodhi* and *sattva*. *Bodhi*, which means "enlightened," is derived from the same word that gives us *Buddha*. *Sattva* means "sentient being." A sentient being is any being with consciousness or the potential to become conscious. Animals and insects are sentient beings, while plants are not. A bodhisattva is a person who dedicates his life to the enlightenment of all other sentient beings in the universe. Sometimes this word is translated as "enlightening being" because bodhisattvas are dedicated to the "enlightening" of all other sentient beings. Some bodhisattvas are exceptionally great beings who can manifest at will for the good of others. Other bodhisattvas are merely ordinary people who have made the extraordinary vow to dedicate themselves to the well-being of others. The *Sutra of the Eight Realizations of Great Beings* is directed mainly at such ordinary bodhisattvas. It is intended to teach them how to behave in the world, and how to help others. It teaches that the life of a bodhisattva must be characterized by compassion, caring, wisdom, and kindness. In this sutra, as well as in many others, the Buddha explains that the bodhisattva path is an active path that leads into life, not a passive way that seeks only to retreat from life.

Buddhism is an eminently practical religion because it teaches us how to live in this world. It is also the most mystical of religions because it shows us how to experience transcendental awareness in every moment of our lives. The Buddha is sometimes called "the great doctor" because he shows us how to cure ourselves of the ills of ignorance. He is sometimes called "the great teacher" because he teaches us how to free ourselves from the greed and anger that bind us to the world. He is sometimes called "the great ox" because he uses his strength to draw us toward the truth. In the *Sutra of the Eight Realizations of Great Beings*, the Buddha summarizes the principal points of his teaching. As its introductory verse says, this sutra ideally should be "held in the mind, and chanted often, both night and day."

THE TRANSLATOR AND THE TRANSLATION

All Buddhist sutras originally were talks given by the Buddha between the years of 463–383 BCE. They were remembered in a vibrant and complex oral tradition for hundreds of years before they were set down in writing. Though the Buddha spoke a language called Old Maghadi, his teachings were first recorded in the Sanskrit and Pali languages because these languages had well-developed writing systems. A written record of a talk by the Buddha is generally known as a sutra. The word *sutra,* from which we derive the English word *suture,* means "stitched together." Very early Buddhist sutras were recorded on palm leaves and stitched together. Once they were written down, the sutras were carried to areas outside of the Buddhist world and translated into many other languages, including Central Asian languages, Chinese, Tibetan, Mongolian, and many others. Korea and Japan used Chinese versions of the sutras throughout most of their histories. Only a portion of the entire collection of Buddhist sutras has been translated into English. Buddhist literature is voluminous because of the large number of talks given by the Buddha, who taught for forty-five years. The spread of Buddhism through Asia generally followed established trade routes. After leaving the Ganges River valley, it spread north into Kashmir and Central Asia via the silk road. It began to enter China from the oasis states of Central Asia that lie to China's west. Buddhist sutras and teachers also entered China via sea routes from India.

The translator of the *Sutra of the Eight Realizations of Great Beings* was a Parthian monk, whose name in Chinese is An Shih-kao. His Parthian name is unknown. He probably traveled through Central Asia to arrive in China in 148 CE. Since the Parthians were excellent sailors, it is also possible that he traveled to China by sea. Parthia was a large kingdom located to the south of the Caspian Sea in what is now Iran. The English language has preserved some memory of Parthia in the phrase "Parthian shot." A Parthian shot is an shot delivered while in flight, or in feigned flight, from an enemy. This phrase originally was used to describe the fighting style of Parthian soldiers who shot their arrows while riding on horses.

An Shih-kao is reported to have been a Parthian prince who renounced royal life to enter a Buddhist monastery. He is said to have had superb linguistic abilities. He made his translations in Loyang, one of China's ancient capitals, and now the city of Xian. An Shih-kao is said to have translated over one hundred sutras into Chinese, but only about twenty or thirty of them exist today. He is the most important early translator of Buddhist sutras into Chinese. In addition to the *Sutra of the Eight Realizations of Great Beings,* he is known to have translated parts of the *Abhidharma,* which contains the basic teachings of Buddhism. He is the first person to teach Buddhist meditation techniques in China. There are many stories about An Shih-kao's psychic and paranormal abilities. He is said to have been able to communicate with animals. Chinese records show that he left Loyang to travel south in 170 CE. It is not known what became of him after that.

FOR ALL DISCIPLES OF THE BUDDHA

This sutra is different from all other Buddhist sutras because it does not begin with the line: "Thus have I heard, at one time, the Buddha was in such and such a place before a gathering of people..." As mentioned earlier, An Shih-kao may have decided that the sutra would be more accessible to his Chinese audience if he left its introductory passage out. A normal introduction to a Buddhist sutra always says who was present at the talk, what was said, when it was said, where it was said, and who remembered it.

The verse at the beginning of the sutra must stand as its introduction: *For all disciples of the Buddha: morning and night, hold them in your mind, and chant them often, these eight realizations of great beings.* This verse is clearly asking us to chant the sutra at least once every morning and night. Chanting a sutra is a common and very beneficial practice for it steadies the mind, brings peace to our homes, reminds us of the Dharma, and helps us focus our energies on things that matter. Many people also believe that chanting confers mystical benefits on its practitioners because the words of the Buddha contain a power that is released by reverently voicing them. Chanting can also be thought of as a comparatively active sort of meditation. Properly done, it can produce meditative states that are as deep and as beneficial as those produced by silent meditation. Chanting is an especially important part of Buddhism as it is practiced in China.

This verse is directed to "all disciples of the Buddha." A "disciple of the Buddha" is someone who has formally taken refuge in Buddhism and accepted Shakyamuni Buddha as his teacher. Others may respect Buddhism and learn from the teachings of the Buddha, but they are not truly disciples until they have actually taken refuge. Needless to say, this does not mean that non-Buddhists cannot learn from this, or any other, Buddhist sutra. Very few people would decide to become Buddhists without first understanding what the teachings mean.

When a sutra is chanted, we must have the right attitude. Just as beautiful music cannot be played on an instrument that is out of tune, so we cannot receive the full benefit of chanting if our attitudes are confused, self-centered, suspicious, close-minded, or condescending. Before chanting we should settle our minds as if in meditation. We should then approach the words of the

Buddha with the utmost sincerity. We should think of him as our friend and teacher, as someone who wants to help us. Then with great concentration, we should chant the sutra. We may chant alone or in a group, and we may chant loudly or softly. Once we have chanted the same sutra enough times to be used to its particular rhythms, we should strive to make our voices sound musical, but slightly monotonous, like the sea coming in and going out, coming in and going out. This kind of sound pattern has a very restful effect on the entire being. In part we are actively speaking, and in part we are resting and going deeper into the meditative states on which all higher wisdom is founded. In times when we are not chanting, we should reflect on the meaning of the sutra and allow its import to reverberate in our minds and throughout our lives. As the sounds of chanting permeate our memories, the peace and wisdom they evoke will accompany us in everything that we do.

THE FIRST REALIZATION

The Nature of This World

Realize that this world is impermanent, that nations are unsafe and unstable, that the four elements cause suffering and are empty, and that there is no self within the five skandhas; that all things that arise must change and decline, and that they are but false appearances without any stable essence; that the mind is the source of evil, and that form is a congregation of wrongdoings.

Contemplate all of this, and gradually you will disentangle yourself from the cycle of birth and death.

THE SUTRA OF THE EIGHT REALIZATIONS OF GREAT BEINGS CAN BE divided into two parts. The first part is the first realization, while the second part is the remaining seven. This first realization is concerned with the Buddha's analysis of this world; in this realization he discusses impermanence, emptiness, the nature of mind, and the cycle of birth and death. The purpose of this discussion is to make us understand the nature of the world that we live in. In the seven realizations that follow this one, the Buddha will teach us how to live in the world. The most important ideas in the first realization are impermanence and emptiness. I will discuss these ideas in greater detail below.

IMPERMANENCE

Realize that this world is impermanent, that nations are unsafe and unstable.

The Buddha's explanation of life in this world is founded on the idea of impermanence. He taught that everything changes and that nothing stays the same. The Buddha emphasized impermanence not to discourage us, but to make us realize the true nature of existence. If we understand that everything is impermanent, we will behave differently than if we mistakenly believe that this world is not subject to constant change.

The Buddha concludes the *Diamond Sutra* by saying, "All phenomena are like dreams, like bubbles, like shadows. They are like dew, like lightning. And they should be contemplated as such." The images used in this very famous string of metaphors are images of impermanence. By saying that all phenomena are like dreams, bubbles, shadows, dew, or lightning, the Buddha is saying in a graphic way that all phenomena change, and that they change quickly. Dreams come and go, bubbles pop, dew evaporates in the sun, and lightning only flashes for a second. Nothing stays the same. All things change.

In the *Sutra of Great Wisdom* the Buddha says, "This world is impermanent. It is like the moon in the water. All that we do is torn asunder by the winds of change." Again, he is not trying to dishearten us with this statement. He is just telling us how it is. The moon in the water is beautiful, and we may enjoy it as long as it lasts, but no one should believe that it is permanent. We cause ourselves to suffer whenever we attempt to cling to the phenomena of this world, which by their very natures are evanescent. Everything is torn asunder by the winds of change.

There is an old story that well illustrates the importance of accepting change. Once during the time of the Buddha there was a wealthy woman whose only child died suddenly. The woman was so anguished by her son's death that she carried him in her arms into the street where she frantically asked anyone who would listen to her if they knew of some way to bring him back to life. People only looked at her with sadness as they shook their heads. At last she came upon someone who told her to go see the Buddha. "Maybe he can help you," the person said. With that advice, the woman rushed to where the Buddha was staying and asked him if he could help her.

The Buddha said, "To save this child you will need four or five mustard seeds. And you must obtain these seeds from a family that has never known death."

The woman rushed back onto the street and began going from house to house asking if she could have some mustard seeds. The seeds themselves were easy to obtain, but no one could say that their family had not known death. At last she gave up searching and went back to the Buddha. When she saw him again she noticed that he wore an expression of profound compassion, and with that she understood that nothing is permanent and that everyone must die. At last she was ready to give up her futile attachment to a child who already was gone.

People change, phenomena change, our thoughts, dreams, feelings, ideas, and lives change all the time. Nothing stays the same. The *Treatise on the Perfection of Great Wisdom* says that change occurs in two basic ways: from moment to moment, and over longer periods of successive or continuous change. Momentary change is apparent all around us. The wind blows, sounds come and go, our hearts beat, our eyes blink—everything in us and around us changes from moment to moment. Successive change is also apparent all around us, but some thought is required to see it. Successive change means a continuous accumulation of momentary changes in something that we normally think of as enduring over time, such as a nation, a geological formation, a sports team, a traditional way of doing something, a language. As the years go by, a vast number of momentary changes accumulate in such entities. Eventually, they will not even resemble their original states. The erosion of sea coasts or the evolution of species on earth are also good examples of successive change. In the moment we do not notice these changes, but over time they are very large. When the Buddha says that *nations are unsafe and unstable*, he is referring to the idea of successive change.

The *Madhyanta-vibhaga-tika* says that change can be understood as being universal to all phenomena by understanding that no phenomenon stands alone. All phenomena depend on other phenomena, and thus when any one of them changes, all of them change.

Once we are convinced that all things change, there are two basic ways that we can use this information. We can use it to prepare ourselves to accept that which we must accept, and we can use it to inspire ourselves to look toward the future with a hopeful and positive attitude. Most people feel gloomy when they contemplate the truth of impermanence because they only imagine good things turning to bad. But just as good things can turn to bad, so also can bad things turn to good. Change leads us out of difficult situations, it relieves us of our cares, and it is the process by which we transform ourselves into Buddhas. If nothing changed, we would never grow.

All things that arise must change and decline, and they are but false appearances without any stable essence. This means that if we believe that anything has a stable essence or that it is not subject to change, we are being distracted from the truth by a false appearance. All things that arise must change.

The concept of change or impermanence is important in and of itself, but it is also important because the Buddha used this concept to explain an even deeper idea that is even more central to his teaching. If we can grasp what the Buddha meant by successive change in a nation or along a coast line, we should also be able to grasp that the book we are holding, the chair we are sitting on, and the clothes we are wearing are subject to successive change as well. We should be able to see that everything for which we have a word or a concept is subject to successive change. Though the things of our world may seem substantial, when we think about them deeply we can see that they are essentially evanescent and that they cannot really ever be grasped or held. All that we can hold onto is a false appearance that is fundamentally devoid of all absolute qualities.

In the *Diamond Sutra* the Buddha asserts that even our minds have no essence that can be grasped when he says, "The mind of the past cannot be grasped, the mind of the present cannot be grasped, and the mind of the future cannot be grasped." This succinct truth has the unique quality of being both self-evident and difficult to grasp!

The concept of impermanence goes hand in hand with the Buddha's teachings on emptiness. Emptiness means that nothing has a permanent "self-nature" or essence. Since everything changes all the time, nothing can be said to be any more substantial than the moon reflected on the water, or the dew on the morning grass, or the dream that just eluded us.

EMPTINESS

The second important idea in this first realization is the idea of emptiness. *Realize... that the four elements cause suffering and are empty, and that... all things... are but false appearances without any stable essence.* Just as all things always change, so no thing has a stable essence. Just as nothing stays the same, so everything is empty.

Emptiness is a special term in Buddhism. It means "having no permanent, definite, or absolute aspect whatsoever." The Buddha taught that everything within the phenomenal universe is empty. Nothing within it has any permanent, definite, or absolute aspect whatsoever. Nothing has any stable essence. If one wants to understand the teachings of the Buddha, it is as important to understand emptiness as it is to understand impermanence.

Buddhist thinkers sometimes say that there are six basic ways to understand emptiness. The first is to understand that our sense organs are empty. The second is to understand that everything our sense organs perceive is empty. The third is to understand that the interaction between our sense organs and what they perceive is empty. The fourth is to understand that the concept of emptiness itself is empty. The fifth is to understand that everything in the universe is empty. The sixth is to understand that there is no permanent aspect anywhere beyond the reaches of the universe, no matter how we may conceive of what the universe is.

None of this says that the world is not here, or that nothing exists, or that we must despair of our condition. Emptiness simply means that nothing has an unchanging essence or self-nature that is independent of other things. To believe otherwise is to be deluded.

The *Treatise on the Perfection of Great Wisdom* says, "Since phenomena arise due to extrinsic causes and conditions, they do not have a self-nature, and thus they are empty."

The *Sutra of Magnificent Mysteries* says, "Without emptiness, there is no form. Without form, there is no emptiness. The two are like the moon and the light of the moon: From first to last they are always together."

Emptiness is a far-reaching idea that has many profound consequences. When we understand emptiness, we change the way we live and the way we feel. When we do not understand emptiness, we tend to cling to things and have strong emotional reactions to what are really only transitory appearances. The concept of emptiness flies in the face of basic human psychology, for one of our strongest tendencies is to treat ourselves, other people, and the things of the world as if they were permanent, enduring entities that can and should be imbued with all of the significance our passion would like them to have. The Buddha reminds us *that all things that arise must change and decline, and that they are but false appearances without any stable essence* to help us see beyond the delusions of our minds and our indefatigable tendency to project our own psychic data onto the world around us. Emptiness is both a philosophical term and a practical technique for overcoming the delusions of this world. The Buddha intended us to understand it in both ways.

While emptiness is a profound philosophical idea, it is also something that can be experienced. Direct perception of the emptiness and unity of all things is the theme of many Ch'an stories. Deep understanding of emptiness helps us maintain a sense of reverence for everything that happens to us. The following story took place in the nineteenth century.

Once Master Isan was getting ready to take a bath. Since the bath water was too hot, he asked a disciple to bring him a bucket of cold water. The disciple came with the cold water and added enough to bring the temperature of the bath down. Then he threw the remaining water on the ground.

Isan said, "Why are you being so wasteful? Everything has value and everything should be appreciated for what it is. Instead of throwing that water away, you could have used it to water our plants. Even a single drop of water has infinite value if you truly understand how rare and wonderful it is, and how it is interconnected with all other things in the universe."

After hearing this, the disciple experienced a small awakening and decided to change his name to "Water Drop." Later in life, this disciple became the famous Japanese master, Master Tekisui (1822–99), whose name means "Water Drop." Master Tekisui was respected by everyone who knew him.

Many years after the incident described above, Tekisui was preaching the Dharma when he was asked by one of his listeners, "What is the most precious thing in the universe?"

Tekisui replied, "A drop of water."

Then another listener asked him, "If emptiness subsumes all things in the universe, what subsumes emptiness?"

Tekisui replied simply, "A drop of water."

Master Tekisui understood that since the mind is one with all things, it is also one with a single drop of water, and the drop of water is one with all. When we truly understand emptiness, our minds are freed from the constraints of believing in an impossible essence or a rigid permanence among things. In this freedom they are able to soar to the highest heights, to expand beyond all limits, or to see the universe in a single drop of water. When emptiness is fully understood, our minds grow beyond the confinements that hold us fixed in a deluded assessment of the conditions of our lives. The teachings of the Buddha are at once practical, philosophical, and mystical, for to experience his teachings is to experience life as you never have before.

THE EMPTINESS OF THE FOUR ELEMENTS

The four elements are the four basic material components of the phenomenal universe according to the ancients: earth, water, fire, and wind. In modern English when we say "the material world," we are essentially talking about the same thing that the Buddha was talking about in his discussions of the four elements. When the Buddha says *the four elements cause suffering and are empty,* he is saying that all material phenomena are without any stable essence and that to believe otherwise is to suffer. There is nothing that does not change and nothing that can be clung to. Everything is empty. When we mistakenly believe that we can discover absolutes within the four elements, we will begin to create conditions that will lead to suffering for the simple reason that we are wrong.

A human body is comprised of earth, water, fire, and wind. Some parts of us are solid (earth), some are liquid (water), we must heat ourselves (fire), and we must breathe (wind). If any one of these parts were to become weak, we would become sick.

If any one of these parts were suddenly to withdraw from us, we would die. Plants can also be understood in this way, for plants must grow in the earth, they must be watered, they must have sunshine, and they must have air. If any of these elements is missing, a plant will quickly die. From a scientific point of view, the four elements can be understood as representing the three basic states of matter—solid, liquid, and gas—and the heat which causes them to move between one state and another. From a Buddhist point of view, the four elements are the four basic states of deluded awareness. Just as there is no stable essence within the false appearances of the phenomenal world around us, so there is no stable essence within the four elements. The *Sutra of the Child with Good Thoughts* says, "The four elements are empty, and they are nothing but empty... when they combine they are like the trace left by a bird flying in the sky."

The four elements cause suffering when we fail to understand that they are both impermanent and empty. When we fail to understand the true nature of the world we live in, we suffer. When we cling to dreams or ideas that have no true essence or self-nature, we set ourselves up to feel disappointment and pain.

There is an old story that illustrates this point in an interesting way. Once in a very remote part of China, there lived an old couple who were quite well off. They had a lot of land, a big house, and plenty of money. The couple was not happy, though, because they had not been able to have children. They asked everyone they could why they were unable to have children, but no one in that region was able to tell them. Then one day a young Buddhist monk who had only recently entered the order visited their village. The old couple was delighted at his appearance, and they asked him to their house so they could feed him and pay their respects to him. After he had eaten, they asked him to speak about the Dharma and explain to them why they were unable to have children. Since the monk was young and not knowledgeable about Buddhism, he was not sure how to answer them. As the couple waited expectantly, he became more and more nervous about what to say.

As his silence persisted, the old couple, who mistook his reticence for wisdom, proceeded to bow down before him. They touched their foreheads to the floor and waited for him to speak. The young monk, who had no idea what to say, began to feel very uncomfortable. In his anxiety, he began to think that it was a lot harder to be a monk than he had first realized. Here were two people imploring him to explain something he knew nothing about. In his consternation, he exclaimed, "How difficult!"

When the couple heard him say that, they breathed a sigh of relief for they understood him to be describing their situation, not his. It had been difficult! All those years they had tried to have children, but nothing had ever come of it. In gratitude, they raised and lowered their heads in a series of short bows before him.

When the monk saw the effect his words had had on the couple, and that his attempt to find relief from his situation had only worsened it, he became so anxious he began to perspire. What was he to do? If he said nothing he would disappoint the couple, and yet if he said something he would only expose his ignorance. Thinking simply of himself, he said, "Such suffering!"

When the old couple heard this, they again were relieved, for here was someone who really understood them! For years they had tried to have children, yet they had never met with success. Truly that was suffering! As they absorbed the fullness of his remarks, the old couple began to weep uncontrollably where they knelt on the floor. All those years, and now at last, someone

...truly understood their plight! As the couple continued to weep, the young monk thought to himself that the situation was going from bad to worse. In a state of great anxiety, he quietly left the room.

The couple cried together for a long time. Then they waited quietly and reverently for the young monk to continue, but when they did not hear his voice for a long time, they at last raised their heads to see that he was gone.

"Oh wonder!" they exclaimed, for they were so overwhelmed by their experience that they were sure the monk had been a living Buddha sent especially to them to explain the truth of suffering. "What a wonder!" they exclaimed as they absorbed the deep meaning of his profound message. And from that day on, they worried less about what they did not have and much more about what they could give to others. Their practice of the Dharma improved, for their understanding of the nature of phenomenal existence at last was built upon the truth. And with this truth they found joy, because they no longer invested all of their hopes in the evanescent world of phenomenal change.

The Buddha taught the truths of impermanence and emptiness not to hurt us or make us sad, but to help us rid ourselves of the deluded thinking that binds us to things we cannot have, or cannot have for long. Understanding impermanence and emptiness can save us from much suffering and hardship, for these truths can help us look beyond the "false appearances" of things into the deep nature of life that alone is real.

THE EMPTINESS OF SELF

After claiming that the four elements are empty, the Buddha adds that *there is no self within the five skandhas*. This means that the self or the personality is empty. Just as all things, all ideas, all phenomena, and all phenomenal states are empty, so too are all people. Just as there is no "stable essence" within phenomena, so there is no "stable essence," "soul," or "enduring "self" within people. The five *skandhas* are the five stages of awareness that make up what we normally call individual awareness or individual consciousness. Just as the four elements are empty, so too are the five skandhas. Our bodies tempt us to believe that there is some "stable essence" of a self within us. The Buddha said there is no such essence. Our bodies are just like other phenomena. They arise due to a complex set of conditions, they abide for a time wholly dependent on other sets of conditions, and then they sicken and die. There is nothing permanent within them. The permanence and fulfillment that we all long for cannot be found in the body, in the self, or in the illusion of having a soul. The Buddha taught that true spiritual fulfillment can only be found after we have overcome these delusions. Though this truth may sound harsh to some, it is not, for the panoramas that open before the mind after the notion of a "self within the five skandhas" has been given up are far more wondrous than anything that was seen before.

The word *skandha* is a Sanskrit word that means "heap." The five skandhas are the heaps of psycho-perceptual data that make up the world of delusion. Sometimes the five skandhas are called "the five yin" in Chinese. They are called yin (versus yang) because they "cover" or "hide" the inherent clarity of the enlightened mind.

The five skandhas are form, sensation, perception, mental activity, and individual awareness. They are the building blocks, or the five basic stages, of deluded awareness. Though the five skandhas are entrancing, and though we normally think of them as being an important part of us, in truth, there is no enduring individual or self within them. They are a series of phenomenal events that lack an agent. They merely hold the appearance of a self within them. They are wholly conditioned by other phenomena and thus they are empty. The Buddha explained deluded awareness in more than one way. Sometimes he explained it by talking about the nature of existence; sometimes he explained it by talking about the nature of perception. And sometimes he explained it by describing the five skandhas. The five-skandha explanation of delusion is his briefest and most succinct description. It was aimed at his most perceptive students. It is a sort of psychology of deluded awareness.

The *Great Commentary on the Five Skandhas* says, "Why did the Buddha teach the five skandhas? He taught them to help us cure three forms of delusion and all that follows from them. The three forms of delusion are: the delusion of having a self-nature, the delusion of having a self that perceives, and the delusion of having a self that acts."

The *Treatise on the Completion of Truth* says, "The sense of self that arises with the five skandhas is based on the body and the belief that the body is real; in truth, there is no self within the skandhas and that is why they are called conditioned skandhas."

The five-skandha explanation is a behavioral/perceptual analysis of the workings of our everyday minds. The Buddha said that the workings of this mind are almost always deluded because people fall into the trap of believing that there is an agent or a self lurking within them, and that this agent or self is the ultimate beneficiary of all that the mind does. The five-skandha explanation of this mistaken notion about the mind is intended to deconstruct the foundation upon which this mistake rests. If we can see our minds for what they are, the Buddha said, we will know how to use them to help rather than harm the world we live in. When we do not understand them for what they are, we tend to become selfish and to be motivated by greed, anger, and ignorance. I will discuss each of the five skandhas in more detail below.

The first skandha is form. A form can be anything that stimulates or gives rise to the second skandha, sensation. A form can be an object, a sound, a smell, a taste, a touch, a memory, a thought, a dream, or anything else that stimulates further mental activity.

The second skandha is sensation. Following the appearance of a form, there is a sensation that the form is either agreeable, disagreeable, or neutral.

The third skandha is perception. Perception follows the sensation of a form.

The fourth skandha is mental activity. Once a form has been perceived, mental activity begins. Memories arise, reactions begin, behavioral habits start functioning. Each unit of mental activity can itself be analyzed as a form. Taken all together, these myriad forms of mental activity make up a whole that is quite complex. Upon this whole is built the last skandha—individual awareness.

Individual awareness is based upon the four skandhas that precede it. Since it is itself a complex construction that is dependent on many parts, the Buddha said that it is empty. Though we may believe that our individual awareness is real and that it endures over time, a clear understanding of the four skandhas that underlie it should show us that it is not a self-contained entity that endures over time. It is a "false appearance," a delusion. Our minds create the worlds we live in.

The Buddha said that the five skandhas follow one another with great rapidity. The process of moving from the first skandha to the fifth takes just a fraction of a second. The picture that we have of a world around us and in us is constructed out of a snow storm of rapidly appearing and disappearing skandhas. These skandhas, or moments of cognition, cluster not around a self but around a stream of intention that produces the false appearance of a self. This false self is constantly recreating itself out of the intentional "materials" of greed, anger, and ignorance. The world that we see is a product of our own minds.

One day the great Ch'an master Hui Neng (638–713) visited Fa Hsing Temple in Canton, China. In the temple courtyard he saw two monks arguing heatedly about something. Hui Neng drew closer and heard that they were arguing about a flag that was flying above the temple gate.

Hui Neng heard one monk say, "If there were no wind, then how could the flag move?"

The other monk replied, "If the flag were not moving how would you know that there was any wind? Don't you see? It is the flag that is moving, not the wind."

Hui Neng, who had drawn close to the monks by this time, said, "It is neither the flag that is moving, nor the wind that is moving. It is only your minds that are moving."

The *Treatise on the Perfection of Great Wisdom* says, "Sentient beings arise out of the five skandhas and the conditions that underlie them."

The *Ekkotarika-agama* says, "The Buddha said that the skandha of form is like foam, the skandha of sensation is like a bubble, the skandha of perception is like a wild horse, the skandha of mental activity is like a banana tree, and thus the skandha of individual awareness is nothing more than an illusion." The Buddha said that the skandha of mental activity is like a banana tree because a banana tree is comprised of leaves curled together in the shape of a trunk. It looks substantial, but it is not, and therefore the skandha of individual awareness is "nothing more than an illusion," since it is entirely based on this. If we peel it apart, we find that nothing is there, that it is empty.

The *Sutra of the Victorious King* compares the skandhas to a house. We seem to inhabit them and draw comfort from them, but in truth their "shelter" is more like a prison than a home.

The *Treatise on the Perfection of Great Wisdom* compares the five skandhas to demons, for it is the skandhas that heap suffering upon us and keep us confined to the painful cycle of birth, sickness, old age, and death.

Seeing through the five skandhas is not a mere intellectual exercise. It is both a profound experience and one of the principal goals of all Buddhist practice. The following passage comes from the autobiography of one of China's most influential monks, Master Han Shan (1546–1623). In this passage he describes what he saw the first time the delusion of the five skandhas fell away. The scene takes place on Wu-t'ai Mountain, which is located in north China: "One day after finishing my meal, I suddenly entered a deep meditative state. In this state, I perceived neither my body nor my mind. All I could see were the five great lights of deep consciousness. The tranquility of this state was awesome, and the world appeared in it as if it were being reflected in a great mirror. The mountains, rivers, and plains were imbued with a brilliant lucidity that had awareness, and yet when I looked for my body or mind, I could not find them anywhere."

When we see beyond the five skandhas, the container self, which confines the fullness of human consciousness, is washed away and the world appears "as if reflected in a great mirror."

The five great lights of deep consciousness are the profound forces that underlie the four elements plus emptiness.

THE MIND IS THE SOURCE OF EVIL

The Buddha often explained emptiness and impermanence by getting people to think about how phenomena arise, change, and decline. The process of arising, changing, and declining is a general form of the cycle of birth and death. Birth corresponds to arising while death corresponds to declining. The purpose of these explanations is to make us focus on the details of change, and thereby realize that nothing is permanent. When we completely understand that nothing is permanent and that nothing has a "stable essence," we will understand that all appearances to the contrary are but "false appearances." A false appearance is any phenomena that we mistakenly believe is not empty.

When the Buddha says that sentient beings are "deluded," he means that they accept "false appearances" as being wholly real. The Buddha described this state of delusion as being like a dream, but he did not mean that some absolute self or being is doing the dreaming. He meant that no self is dreaming, that the dream is dreaming itself, and that while the dream is dreaming itself, it has no "stable essence." If we can awake from this dream, he said, then we will see that there exists an awareness that is far greater than anything we had imagined before.

Master Ta Chu (dates unknown) of the T'ang Dynasty said, "The mind is the basis of all things... and thus, if you want to understand good and evil, understand your mind."

The *Lankavatara Sutra* says, "All things arise from the mind and all things are extinguished in the mind."

The *Sutra of Bequeathed Teachings* says, "If you can control your mind, you can do anything."

Master Ta Chu said, "Those who are wise seek to understand the mind, not the Buddha, while those who are ignorant seek to understand the Buddha, and not the mind. The wise control their minds, while the ignorant control only their bodies."

There is a wonderful Ch'an tale that illustrates how the mind tends to create its own world by grasping at interpretations that are not warranted by the facts. One day Master Ikkyu was traveling with a young monk when the two of them came to a river. On the bank of the river was a young woman who was afraid to cross the waters, which were quite swift and deep. Out of compassion for her, Ikkyu volunteered to carry her across. When they reached the other side, Ikkyu let the young woman down and continued on his journey as before. Nothing more happened that day, but a few months later, the young monk spoke up.

"Master," he said, "There is something that has been bothering me for long time. Can you please help me come to understand it?"

"What is it?" Ikkyu asked.

The young monk said, "Do you remember a few months ago when we crossed that river and you carried the woman on your back? I cannot understand why you did that. Haven't you always taught us to avoid contact with women?"

Ikkyu looked at the young monk and sighed. "Look at you," he said. "Do you see how your mind works? All I did was spend a few minutes carrying someone across a river, but you have been carrying her in your mind for months now!"

All things, both good and bad, start in the mind. Delusion is based on the workings of the mind. The sutra says *realize that...*

the mind is the source of evil, and that form is a congregation of wrongdoings. Forms are nothing more than "false appearances" that we have created in our own minds. The suspicions of the young monk in the story above were solely a product of his own mind. They were wholly disconnected from the true nature of Ikkyu's actions. Whenever we are suspicious, we live in a dark world of our own fears and wrongdoings. Master Ta Chu said "those who are wise seek to understand the mind, not the Buddha" because he knew that enlightenment cannot be given to us by anyone. Even the Buddha cannot purify our minds for us. All he, or anyone else, can do is show us how to help ourselves.

The Buddha says that "the mind is the source of evil" to make us realize that everything we have is of our own making. If we frequently engage in harmful or suspicious thoughts, our lives will become dark and unpleasant. If we frequently engage in beneficial and trusting thoughts, our lives will gradually become brighter and more joyful. Our minds are the turning points of our intentions and, thus, of our karma. There is no evil in the world; there is only evil in our minds. The *Flower Garland Sutra* says, "The mind is a painter. It paints its own world."

The phrase *form is a congregation of wrongdoings* echoes this point. Forms are all of the false appearances that have been generated by our minds. They are described as being wrongdoings because ultimately they have been created from bad intentions within our own minds. They are called a congregation because all delusion is made up of many parts. Delusion is delusion precisely because it is always dependent on many other causes and conditions. Forms appear because there is karma to generate them. There is karma because there is intention. There is a congregation of wrongdoings because our intentions circulate in a mind that seeks to justify itself on its own deluded terms. "The mind is the source of evil" and thus the forms it sees are a "congregation of (its own) wrongdoings."

In the story above, the young monk was given to suspicion and low thoughts about the relations between men and women and so he burdened himself for three whole months. The story below illustrates this same point in another way. Interestingly, this story also involves a river. Once there was a man walking along the bank of a river. As he walked, he watched a boatman push his boat into the water to prepare to take some people across the river. Just then a Ch'an master happened on the scene. The man stepped forward and said, "Master, I just watched that boatman push his boat into the water. When he did that he must have killed some of the crayfish and mussels that live at the water's edge. Who is to blame for their deaths? Is the boatman at fault or are his passengers to blame?"

The Ch'an master answered, "It is neither the boatman's fault nor the passengers' fault."

Confused by this answer the man, asked, "If it is not their fault, then whose fault is it?"

The Ch'an master replied, "It is your fault."

THE FOUR CONTEMPLATIONS

The first realization of the *Sutra of the Eight Realizations of Great Beings* is concerned with what is generally called the Buddha's view of this world. This first realization is a description of the basic features of the world we live in. The points made in this realization are made in many other Buddhist sutras. The Buddha emphasized these basic points on many different occasions because it is essential that we have a correct understanding of the conditions of our lives if we are to know how to apply the rest of the Buddha's teachings. Buddhism is a religion of mental clarity. Its practices are based on reason. The central purpose of all Buddhist practice is the attainment of wisdom, or understanding. The Buddha frequently exhorted his followers to think for themselves. All of his teachings were designed to help us help ourselves. Though this point may seem obvious, it quite often gets lost among the details of secondary concerns.

The last line of the first realization says *contemplate all of this and gradually you will disentangle yourself from the cycle of birth and death*. Contemplation is central to all of the Buddha's teachings because mental clarity cannot be achieved without it. The first realization of this sutra contains four of the most important contemplations taught by the Buddha. These contemplations are meant to be used to help us overcome our problems. They should be applied to the actual events of our lives. Before we discuss them in detail, I will briefly say a few words about what the Buddha meant by the cycle of birth and death.

The cycle of birth and death has no beginning and no end. It is a cycle driven by karma and the impure intentions that underlie it. No sooner does one life end than another begins. No sooner does one karmic result wane than another waxes. The Buddha taught that the cycle of birth and death cannot be stopped. We can only hope to "disentangle" ourselves from it. He taught the importance of intention and of cause and effect to help us understand how to disentangle ourselves from both the causes and the effects of our karma. When we understand what it is that causes us to be trapped in the cycle of birth and death, we will also understand how to free ourselves from it. The cycle of birth and death is maintained by narrowed awareness and a continuing fixation on the particulars of that awareness. Selfishness has many names and many possible descriptions, but each of them is founded upon a significant narrowing of awareness and a limiting of our true potential.

The Buddha never asks us to defeat this cycle, or change it, or destroy it. He asks us to disentangle ourselves from it through understanding. His teachings show us how to extirpate ourselves from the passions of greed, anger, and ignorance that bind us to false notions of self, and to the false appearance of its importance. The contemplations mentioned in this first realization are meant to help us fully comprehend the world we live in and the parts that we play in that world. The right way to do the following contemplations is to think about them and apply them to your own life. These contemplations are not meant to be abstract ideals with little connection to our lives, but rather a basis for understanding the fullness of life as we actually live it in this world. As soon as these contemplations lead you to understand how one of their truths may be applied to your life, the right thing to do is apply it immediately. You will reap the benefits of your introspection very quickly. All anyone needs to do to be convinced of the truth of the Dharma is apply it to the life they are living. It always works.

The *Lotus Sutra* says, "The Dharma is so high, it can be difficult for people to understand. However, if we contemplate our own minds, it is easy to understand, for the mind, the Buddha, and sentient beings are all fundamentally one and the same."

The first contemplation mentioned in this sutra is the contemplation on impermanence. This contemplation is indicated by the line *this world is impermanent... nations are unsafe and unstable*. In this contemplation, we reflect on the impermanence of all things, including ourselves. This contemplation has four main purposes: to make us understand the true nature of life in this world; to alert us to the dangers of clinging to phenomenal joys; to make us feel grateful for whatever we have; and to make us want to understand more about who and what we really are. Properly practiced, this contemplation should awaken within us a longing for higher states of awareness. The *Sutra of Vast Meaning* says, "The contemplation on impermanence helps us overcome sloth and laziness." The *Sutra of the Elder Sumagadha* says, "Contemplate that all things are impermanent and that nothing belongs to you... Understand that all things that come together must also come apart."

The second contemplation is the contemplation on emptiness. This contemplation is indicated by the line *the four elements cause suffering and are empty*. This contemplation makes us aware that all things are produced from many other things and that, therefore, no one thing can be clung to. The four elements cause suffering only when we do not realize that they are empty. Once we fully understand that they are empty, they will not make us suffer any more. This contemplation has two basic purposes: to make us realize the true nature of all phenomena, including the phenomena of our own false self, and to help us overcome the difficulties of life, for when we understand the inherent emptiness of our problems, we are better equipped to see through them and not react with passionate or violent emotions. The *Pravara-deva-raja-pariprecha Sutra* says, "Profound contemplation on emptiness takes us far from any individual point of view while it suffuses us with equanimity." The *Sutra on the Practice of Great Wisdom* says, "When we do the contemplation on emptiness, we should do it with our whole mind and not become distracted by anything, for if we are not distracted by anything then our realization will not be tainted with falseness."

The third contemplation is the contemplation on the absence of a true essence, or the absence of a true self. This contemplation is indicated by the line *there is no self within the five skandhas*. This contemplation is roughly the same as the contemplation on emptiness, though it is directed more at the false self of the person than at the phenomena that the person perceives. This contemplation, as does the contemplation on emptiness, recalls the line *all things... are but false appearances without any stable essence*. The *Sutra on the Emptiness of the Five Skandhas* says, "Contemplate the five skandhas and see that there is neither a self within them nor anything that might belong to a self. Then continue contemplating this and realize that in all of the world, there is nothing that you can really grasp or have, and that even the cycle of birth and death is fundamentally an illusion. From self-realizations like these, you will achieve nirvana."

The fourth contemplation is the contemplation on uncleanness. This contemplation is indicated by the line *the mind is the source of evil, and form is a congregation of wrongdoings*. This contemplation is used primarily to overcome unwanted sexual attraction, but it can be used to help us overcome any strong desire. In this contemplation, we reflect on all of the many problems that will arise from our desire. When used to deflect sexual attraction, we consider that the person in question is in many ways a projection of our own minds; then we consider why we have made that projection, that the actual person is both more and less than that projection, that they will become sick and die, that their bodies are filled with half-digested food, waste, and many other unpleasant things. When the object of our desire is a thing, we follow this same general line of thought, but consider that it will cost time or money to obtain what we want, and that one day it will become old or broken down. The purpose of this contemplation is not to make us feel revolted, but only to help us cool our passion. Properly used, it can quickly help us regain a state of even mindedness wherein we can make more thoughtful decisions about whatever it is that has caught our fancy. Again, this contemplation is not designed to make us feel revulsion toward anything, but only to help us regain our balance when we are swept away by strong desires. Try it some time. You will see that it is very effective. The *Treasure Cloud Sutra* says, "Practice the contemplation on uncleanness to cure excessive desire." The *Moon Lamp Samadhi Sutra* says, "The contemplation on uncleanness rids us of greed."

If the four contemplations mentioned above are used often and applied to our lives, the day will come when we will stop making ourselves a victim of our own self-defeating thoughts and behaviors. In the clarity that results from the absence of our customary confusion, we will see that our minds are far more wonderful than we had ever imagined before.

One day Master Yaoshan Weiyen (751–834) was sitting in meditation, when another monk came by. Enchanted by the master's tranquil expression, the monk could not help but ask, "Master, when you sit so peacefully like that, what are you thinking about?"

"I am thinking about not thinking," the master answered calmly.

"How do you think about not thinking?" the monk asked.

"By not thinking," the master replied.

Being able to not think is a reward that follows thinking about the Buddha's teachings for many years.

THE SECOND REALIZATION

Greed Is the Cause of Suffering

Realize that excessive desire causes suffering. The fatigue and troubles of the cycle of birth and death arise from greed and desire. Have few desires, be receptive, and you will be content in body and mind.

THE FIRST REALIZATION OF THIS SUTRA CONCERNS THE BUDDHA'S teachings on the nature of this world. The next seven realizations are concerned with his teachings on the nature of the human mind and how to live in this world. If we understand the principles discussed in the first realization, we will be in a very good position to understand how to apply the teachings of the next seven realizations to our lives.

Though the worlds that we see are fundamentally a product of our own minds, they usually do not appear this way to us. Like images in an intense dream, our perceptions appear to be wholly real to us, and not to have been generated by our own mental activity. For this reason, the Buddha taught many ways to help us comprehend the true nature of life. He taught that we are where we are not by accident or by any act of a supreme intelligence, but only by our own past actions. Buddhism can seem difficult because it places so much responsibility on the individual practitioner. But ask yourself: Can anyone else understand for me? Can anyone else behave for me? Why should I not be responsible for my actions?

In this realization, the Buddha emphasizes excessive desire, or greed. He says: *Realize that excessive desire causes suffering.* Healthy desires include reasonable hunger, a balanced pursuit of shelter and clothing, reasonable social activity, temperate sexuality, and a balanced pursuit of hobbies or other amusements. "Excessive desire" means going beyond these parameters. Sometimes it takes wisdom to know when we are going too far in one direction or another, but for the most part, most of us know where our limits are. When we exceed them, we cause suffering. Reasonable desires do not preoccupy us, and they are not distracting or extreme. If we do not fulfill them, we do not feel that they cannot wait a little longer. Excessive desires strain our health, impair our concentration, and often cause us to become angry or envious. They seduce us into lying both to ourselves and to our friends.

The Buddha taught that excessive desire is a principal cause of our attachment to the false appearances of this world. Coupled with anger and ignorance, excessive desire binds us to the cycle of birth and death, and to the recurring illusions that keep that cycle going. In modern times, there are literally thousands of ways that we can indulge our desires. And yet, who among us has never realized that excess leads to pain? The profound cravings of our beings issue from a level that is far deeper than anything that can be satisfied by sensual gratification. Our deepest longings are an intimation of a truth that transcends all false appearances and all sensory needs. The Buddha taught that the way to find this truth is to understand that the false self is an illusion and that it maintains itself through greed and anger. *Pure Contemplation of the Dharma* says, "Greed is like a wolf, while anger is like an evil dragon."

When we give ourselves over to our desires, they quickly destroy us. When we moderate them, they gradually lead us to the center of our lives. In the storehouse of our deep Buddha mind there lies dormant the realization that we already are complete, and that nothing need be sought. The Buddha taught the Dharma to help us awaken this dormant realization.

There is a story in one of the sutras that illustrates the persistence of habitual desires, even when we have no need for them. Once there was a group of young women returning to their village from a fishing trip along the Ganges River. They carried baskets filled with fish on their backs. On their way home, the evening sky clouded over and the women were forced to seek shelter. Fortunately, a keeper of a flower shop saw them and invited them to stay in his place for the night. His shop was filled with fresh flowers. The women lay down to rest. Though they all were tired from their long day of walking and working along the river bank, not one of them could fall asleep. They were so unaccustomed to the fragrance of the flowers that they could not relax. At last one of them got up and went outside for her basket of fish. She brought it in and placed it in the middle of the room. With the odor of flowers covered by that of dead fish, the women soon fell asleep.

Excessive desire is like the odor of dead fish. We get so used to it that when the pure fragrance of fresh flowers is offered us, we cannot relax. How tragic to remain bound by a habit generated by an illusion! The great poet Su Tung-p'o once wrote, "Human desires are inexhaustible, and yet that which can fulfill them is limited." The way to overcome excessive or misplaced desire is to understand what causes it. When the cause is understood, the cure is much easier to see.

Desires spring from harmful fixations, which are called *kleshas* in Sanskrit. Sometimes kleshas are also called "unwholesome mental functions," "defilements," "impurities," "obstacles," "deceptions," or "karmic entanglements." Harmful fixations are selfish emotional or mental fixations that spring from greed, anger, or ignorance, and which cause us to harm other sentient beings. They seduce us into treating others with contempt in a vain attempt to raise ourselves above them, or to gratify ourselves at their expense. Nothing good ever comes of giving in to a harmful fixation.

The *Questions of Shakra Sutra* says, "Because there is love and hate, therefore there are harmful fixations… fixations of love and hate arise from our positive and negative feelings toward things." The *Sutra on Comprehending Great Wisdom* says, "The way to end harmful fixations is to be diligent and learn to base your actions on right thought." The *Sutra of Supreme Mindfulness* says, "Harmful fixations, though heaped like mountains, can be torn down by quiet introspection." The *Flower Garland Sutra* says, "All sentient beings are possessed of innumerable harmful fixations." The *Sutra of Great Treasures* says, "Harmful fixations are like wild beasts for they act only in their own interests and won't be controlled." The *Treatise on the Perfection of Great Wisdom* says, "Wisdom is like a good arrow, for it slays harmful fixations."

Harmful fixations can be anything from conscious desires to unconscious urges. When we are conscious of our fixations, they are generally easier to control than when we are not conscious of them. When we are not conscious of them, they are like seeds that lie within the soil of our being. When conditions are right, they grow into the tangled vines of desire. When conditions are not right, they lie dormant, often giving no sign of their presence. Harmful fixations can also be compared to rooms within the unconscious mind. When conditions are right, the doors to these rooms open and the urges behind them come forth. When conditions are not right, the doors remain closed, often giving us no indication of what lies inside. No one can escape these truths. Our minds are filled with a complexity of desire and passion that requires great effort to comprehend, let alone to control and overcome. Desire can be controlled by honest introspection and honest application of the truths revealed thereby. It cannot be controlled by indulgence because indulgence always plants more seeds of the same type.

There is an old story that illustrates the destructiveness of unbridled greed with convincing directness. Once there were two good friends named Chang and Wang. One day when they were taking a walk together they found a large piece of gold. Since they both had seen it at the same time, they decided to divide the piece of gold evenly between them.

Then Chang said to Wang, "The god of our city must have left this gold for us to find. Before we divide it, we should make an offering at the temple to show our gratitude."

Wang replied, "You are right. Why don't you go buy some food for our offering while I go to the temple to prepare things there?"

Both men were very happy, but soon a small demon began stirring in their minds. As Chang walked to the market, he thought to himself: if Wang gets half of this gold, there will be less for me! As Wang walked to the temple, he thought to himself: if I had all of the gold for myself it would last much longer!

From these initial thoughts, terrible events were to follow, for the mind determines everything. Chang purchased a vial of poison with the food, while Wang concealed an axe near the table where they would eventually dine. Each of them thought that his well-being was more important than the life of another.

After they had completed their offering, they took the food out back to eat it, as was the custom in their town. As Chang emptied his vial of poison into the soup, Wang's axe fell on his head. With Chang safely dead, Wang decided that he might as well enjoy some soup before he left with the gold. Before he had consumed half of it, his abdomen was shot through with mortal pain and he died in the dirt beside the body of his former friend.

From the moment they formed the thought to kill one another, both men planted the seeds of their own demises. Their retribution was especially swift and fitting. Had they controlled their greed, they could have lived for many years and enjoyed their good fortune. As it was, they lost everything. Happiness and prosperity can only be safely based on honesty and compassion. When greed enters the mix, the very same things that were a cause for joy quickly become a cause for sadness. The *Sutra of the All-seeing Buddha Eye* says, "The cycle of birth and death is like rushing river rapids, or like waves in the sea." When we give in to base desires, we are pulled into swift currents over which we have very little control. The *Commentary on the Sutra of*

Golden Light says, "Greed is like an ocean current that flows without ceasing."

Harmful fixations are often described in Buddhist literature as impediments or hindrances because they block our view of the truth and prevent us from seeing our own Buddha nature. Sometimes, too, they are described as "deceptions" because they mislead us so easily. When they are described as deceptions, they are usually divided into two basic groups—deceptions of outlook and deceptions of thought or personality. Deceptions of outlook are our philosophies of life. They are wrong views. Wrong views quickly lead to wrong thoughts and wrong actions. They are the ultimate source of many secondary harmful fixations. Wrong views are basically those views that contradict the teachings of the Buddha. Deceptions of thought or personality are the internalized false appearances of the false self. They are nothing more than a vast collection of selected memories, self-serving excuses, self-centered fantasies, base intentions, and often violent defense mechanisms. They are what we draw on for most of our worldly behavior. Of course, the human character also contains intimations of enlightenment, love, kindness, joy, and all of the many promptings that lead us toward Buddhahood. The purpose of Buddhist practice is to use this second group of traits to overcome the first group.

Generally, our harmful fixations work together as a group. Few of us have only one of them. People who are greedy also tend to be proud, quick to anger, ignorant of the consequences of their behavior, and doubtful that life could ever hold more for them than what they desire from it. They also tend to have many wrong views. Greedy people often believe that they have only one life to live so they must get all they can while they are able.

They tend to see themselves as alone in the world, or isolated from other beings, and thus they like to build castles that both protect them from their fears and impress others with their majesty. All of this behavior is fundamentally based on a mistaken understanding of the true nature of life in this world.

The *Sutra in Forty-two Sections* says, "When people give in to their desires, they become enchanted with excess and showing off. They become like a stick of incense that burns itself out; though others may admire its fragrance, the incense itself pays for the spell it casts by destroying itself."

As we examine the roots of our desires, we should consider them in the light of one or more of the contemplations mentioned at the end of chapter 2. These basic contemplations were designed by the Buddha for no other purpose than to help us come to grips with the actual contents of our minds. Properly used, they will save us from much trouble and sadness. When we contemplate the inherent uncleanness of our desires, we will be less likely to be entranced by them. When we contemplate their essential emptiness, we will be less likely to be gulled by their vacuous insistence. When we contemplate the impermanence of both our desires and the conditions that gave rise to them, we will be more inclined to look inward, not outward, for satisfaction.

The *Treatise on the Middle View* says, "When we are wholly selfless, harmful fixations do not arise." The *Sutra of Bequeathed Teachings* says, "People who are afflicted with excessive desires, always think about themselves and thus they have many troubles and cares… Though they may be wealthy, people who have many desires are poor in spirit. Though they may be poor, people who have few desires are rich in spirit."

BE CONTENT IN BODY AND MIND

Excessive desire is cured by its own opposite: balanced awareness. The sutra says: *Have few desires, be receptive, and you will be content in body and mind.* It does not say have no desires. When our desires are balanced and reasonable, we can be content. The Buddha taught that deep wisdom can be found only by following a middle path between dualistic extremes. Too much austerity makes us hard and unsympathetic, while too much indulgence makes us soft and insensitive. Too much desire overstimulates our senses, while too little desire enervates and makes us feel bored. The middle path can always be found by contemplating which side of a dualistic pair is contending for our attention. If we discover that we have begun to fixate on money, we can find a healthy balance again by emphasizing the positive opposites of this fixation: we can practice generosity, spend more time with loved ones, and reflect on the fact that money is valuable only when it helps people, never when it harms them. If we find ourselves becoming fixated on something that makes us angry or resentful, we can find a healthy balance by emphasizing sympathy and compassion. If we are confused by many desires, we can stop and ponder our need to study and learn more.

When we have fewer desires we will be happier because our lives will be easier to manage and we will have more time to consider that which is most important. Honest introspection always leads to the truth. If our introspection leads us to discover many harmful fixations within us, then we must take steps to understand their origins, as we look for ways to balance their deleterious influences. If it leads us to discover inklings of the enlightened Buddha mind within us, then we must encourage these inklings and cause them to grow and become more frequent. There is no better way to counteract the imbalances of samsara than to bathe them in the enlightened wisdom of the Buddha that already lies within us.

Contentment cures greed, sympathy cures anger, and wisdom cures the confusion of many desires arising at once. When we know how to be satisfied with what we have, we can be happy anywhere, and we will always be able to avoid excessive desire and the terrible passions it releases. The *Shurangama Sutra* says, "Wise contentment defeats the demons of the mind." The *Commentary on the Lotus Sutra* says, "Truth is like the sky, meditation like a great cloud, wisdom like the rain." Wisdom is likened to the rain because it washes us and cleans us of our harmful desires. The *Sutra of Supreme Mindfulness* says, "Have few desires, be content, and put to rest all harmful clinging. Disentangle yourself from your attachments, for when you taste greed you are like a fish who swallows a hook."

The following story reminds us that the Buddha can help us only if we are deeply receptive and willing to help ourselves. Once there was a man who was walking on a mountain road. As the dusty miles passed, he became tired and inattentive, and consequently lost his footing and fell down a steep precipice. As he fell, he managed to reach out and grab hold of a tree branch growing out of the cliff. Clutching the branch for dear life, he looked up and down. Far below him were the hard rocks at the bottom of the cliff, while above him there was only the sheer face of the cliff. As far as he could tell there was no way he could save himself. Then he saw the Buddha standing on the road above him. The Buddha was gazing on him with a look of great concern.

The man called out, "Oh Buddha, save me! Save me!"

The Buddha replied, "I will save you, but you must do as I say."

The man cried, "Anything, anything! I will do anything you say!"

"Let go of the branch," the Buddha said.

The man looked down at the rocks at the bottom of the cliff and thought that if he let go of the branch he would surely fall and be killed. His fears made him grab the branch more tightly.

When the Buddha saw that he was not going to let go, he said, "How can I save you if you don't let go?" And with that he turned and left.

THE THIRD REALIZATION

Contentment Is the Source of Happiness

Realize that the mind is insatiable, and that it constantly strives for more, thus adding to its transgressions and mistakes. The bodhisattva is not like this; he thinks often of being satisfied with what he has, and he is peaceful in poverty and upholds the Dharma. Wisdom is his only concern.

The second realization says that excessive desire is the cause of suffering. The third realization says that knowing how to be satisfied with what we have is the cure for that suffering. In this realization, the Buddha explains that contentment is not simply an end in itself, but also a means to an even greater end, for when we are content with what we have and "peaceful in poverty," we will always be able to uphold the Dharma. Contentment allows us to make wisdom our only concern. If we are impatient and dissatisfied with our lives, we will be given to angry moods and to pursuits that waste our energies and only worsen our situation.

This realization applies to all of us, for all of us are "poor" in one way or another. The true definition of a "poor person" is anyone who is so discontented with his circumstances that he has no time to become wise. "Poverty of contentment" is caused most of all by lack of honest introspection. Our minds are "insatiable," as the sutra says, because we do not stop long enough to think about what we are doing. As soon as we have what we once wanted, most of us just want more.

Greed begins in the mind, but it quickly can grow into a monster whose actions ruin many good things. There are seven major problems that arise from having strong desires: They may lead us to steal from others. They may lead us to borrow things and not return them. They may lead us to misappropriate wealth that has been entrusted to us. They may lead us to cheat our business partners through false reporting or through sly methods that lead to our having more control than was originally agreed upon. Strong desires may lead us to misuse company funds, materials, or office supplies. They may lead us to commit acts of extortion or blackmail. Strong desires may lead us to make money by owning or operating enterprises that encourage gambling, the irresponsible use of alcohol or drugs, prostitution, or the killing of animals. The Buddha said that these sorts of professions should be avoided whenever possible.

If we do not know how to be satisfied with what we have and peaceful in poverty, our desires will multiply and grow for many lifetimes. One of China's great Buddhist masters, Master Tao An (312–85), once was given a huge amount of rice by a well-meaning devotee who wanted to help him feed his disciples. The man gave so much rice, however, that Master Tao An hardly had enough room to store it all. When the rice at last had been put away, the master wrote a letter to the man. In it he said, "Thank you very much for the rice you gave us, but I must tell you that your gift has also caused us a lot of trouble because we have no place to put so much!"

Master Tao An understood that having too much can be as big a burden as having too little. He understood that seeking too many things in the world often creates more problems than it solves. When we are in the grip of excessive desire, we focus all of our energy on the sensory world outside of us. As long as that world has arranged itself around us in a way that we like, we will feel happy. The moment things go wrong, however, we will feel sad because we have not developed the inner strength and wisdom to know how to deal with life as it really is. Having excessive desires is part of an early stage in the life process. In this stage, we see ourselves as being at the center of everything. Since we believe that we are all important, our main interest in life is simply to gratify the needs of our "self." At a later stage of development, we will begin to see that the needs and feelings of others are also important and that the exclusive pursuit of our own desires leads only to suffering. We will begin to understand that desire does not really gratify us, but that it actually imprisons us within the walls of an illusion. At a still later stage, we will see that the entire notion of having a separate self is nothing more than a complex collection of false appearances.

Once there was a man riding a mule. When he noticed that there was a man in front of him riding a horse, he began to feel inadequate and jealous. Then he looked behind him and saw another man dragging a cart by his own labor. When he noticed how hard the man behind him was working and how much he was sweating, he began to feel better about himself and his mule.

He said to himself:

> *He's on a horse and I'm on a mule,*
> *and that makes me feel like a fool.*
> *I'm on a mule, but he's on the road,*
> *and that makes me feel soothed.*
> *I'm not as good as him up front,*
> *but at least I'm better than him behind.*

There is a good lesson in this story. If we spend time comparing our lives to those who are "better" than us, we will make ourselves feel jealous and inadequate. If we spend time thinking about those whose circumstances are more difficult than our own, we will inspire ourselves to become sympathetic and compassionate. The Buddha taught that there are five basic ways in which wealth can be lost. It is good to contemplate these five ways because they help us understand that even the most grandiose of circumstances are impermanent. He said that wealth can be taken or destroyed by corrupt government officials, by natural disasters, by criminals, by war, or by wasteful family members. When we have wealth, we should use it to help others. When we share with those who are less fortunate than we are, we help them as we teach ourselves the value of generosity. Wealth that is hoarded away is never really ours anyway. Wealth is really only a significant part of our lives when we use it.

Many years ago in China there was a king who wanted to study under a wise man. The king said to him, "If you accept me as your disciple and come live in my palace, you will always have the best food and clothing. And wherever you go you will ride in a carriage and you will always be accompanied by beautiful women."

The wise man replied that he preferred his life as it was. He said, "When I eat, I eat slowly and thus all of my food tastes good. When I walk, I pay attention to what is around me, and this is every bit as good as riding in a carriage. When I do things, I always think carefully before I act and I don't let myself be carried away by strong feelings, and this is better than the company of even the most beautiful of women."

It is not necessary to be poor to be a good Buddhist. The point of this story, and others like it, is that we should learn to be satisfied with what we have. The Buddha did not teach us to despise wealth or to avoid money. He only taught that wealth should be used for the betterment of the world. When wealth is used for the good of society, it brings pleasure to everyone.

Growth can never be hurried. Words can only serve as aids to our improvement, never as substitutes for life itself. The Buddha taught the Dharma not to tell us what to do, but to help us learn the truth for ourselves. When he advises us to be satisfied with what we have, he is not issuing a command or preaching to us. He is sharing insights gleaned from lifetimes spent in the pursuit of wisdom. Being satisfied with what we have allows us to stop and think, for when we are satisfied, we have time for introspection, and we have time to apply the conclusions of our introspection. The greatest gift any of us has is awareness and the ability to contemplate awareness. To cloud awareness with distractions of greed is as foolish as pouring poison into a lake, or burning a forest to make smoke in the wind. Unlike the eye, awareness can see and know itself. While we would never rub sand in our eyes to improve our vision, why is it that we invite greed into our minds in the hope that it will improve our awareness?

The Dharma is designed to help us stop self-defeating behavior. When we make wisdom our only concern, we begin leading our minds back to their original states of purity and wise innocence. The *Flower Garland Sutra* says, "The teachings of the Buddha are like a great sea. They are entered by faith and crossed by wisdom."

The *Treatise on the Perfection of Great Wisdom* says that great wisdom "is like the rising sun, for it dispels mist and fog. The majesty of great wisdom affects people in two ways—ignorant people are frightened by it, while the wise are delighted... Wisdom does not come from anywhere and it does not go anywhere. The wise know that it cannot be sought among things." The treatise also says that great wisdom is "like vast space, without stain or defilement, without foolishness, or language. When we perceive wisdom in this way, we see the Buddha himself... The reason that Buddhas and bodhisattvas are able to help sentient beings is that their behavior arises out of wisdom."

THE FOURTH REALIZATION

Laziness Leads to Downfall

Realize that laziness leads to downfall. Be diligent and break the hold of harmful fixations. Defeat the four demons and escape the prison of this dark world.

To be lazy is to not do what we know we should do. It is to waste time among sensory pleasures when we know that we should be emphasizing the development of our minds and hearts. The way to overcome negative tendencies is to stress their positive opposites. The way to overcome laziness is to be diligent. The Chinese philosopher Sun Tzu said that in life we are like swimmers in a river that is always flowing against our best interests. If we want to make progress, he said, we must swim against the current, for if we do not, we will be carried downstream. Indeed, just to stay in one place takes effort. The Buddha did not stay still and do nothing. He did not wallow in life's suffering or allow himself to be defeated by the enormity of the world's problems. He taught the Dharma instead. He saw the problem, figured out the solution, and then spent the rest of his life teaching it to others. Kshitigarbha bodhisattva has vowed to remain in hell until all sentient beings have been liberated from it. The energy that lies behind this great vow is based on his knowledge of the positive fulfillment that lies at the end of suffering. Avalokiteshvara bodhisattva has vowed to go to any sentient being who is in need and who calls upon him. When great beings such as these vow to give so much for the good of others, how can the rest of us not vow at least to save ourselves by our own efforts?

Laziness leads to downfall because it is based on ignorance and self-defeating behavior. When we emphasize those things that are negative or frightening in life, we tend to withdraw from the world and to dislike everything that happens to us. When we emphasize those things that are positive in life, we tend to reach out to others and to find pleasure in doing what we know we must do anyway. Negative or lazy ways of thinking tend to be self-fulfilling prophesies. Discouraging thoughts tend to create discouraging outcomes because the conditions that prevail within our minds eventually become manifest in the events of our lives.

There was a time when the Buddha used two monks to talk to people who had become seriously ill. One of the monks was old, while the other was a young man. Before long, people began to notice that when the older monk spoke to the ill they would quickly recover from their diseases, but when the younger monk spoke to them, their condition would only grow worse. The difference lay in what they were saying. The older monk would always say, "Everything is impermanent and so is your disease. If you continue to practice diligently, you will quickly get better." In contrast, the younger monk always said, "Illness is the result of bad karma. There is nothing you can do but accept these conditions and wait for them to pass." The older monk, who had lived longer, had a much deeper understanding of the Buddha's teachings than the younger monk. He knew that once we allow ourselves to feel defeated, our lives can only get even worse.

Diligence is that which helps us "break the hold of harmful fixations" and bad habits. It is based on a deep resolution to become a better person, and not a superficial infatuation with mere concepts of goodness or piety. If we are to delve deeply into our minds, we must be prepared to deal with aspects of ourselves that are less than perfect. If we mistakenly equate diligence with an image of someone else's pious behavior, we will very likely fail to make the deep adjustments that our lives actually require. "Harmful fixations" are harmful, negative tendencies that cause serious problems. Their hold on us is hard to break because these sorts of tendencies are very difficult for most people to recognize. Rather than confront the truth about ourselves, most of us prefer to explain away our behavior or to justify it in a way that makes us feel good but that does not get to the root of the problem.

Paramartha (499–569), who was one of the great early translators of Buddhist texts into Chinese, lived in China during very turbulent times. Paramartha was from northern India. He traveled to South China in 546 to help spread the Dharma. Though he worked in a strange land where he was constantly driven from one place to another by the battles that raged everywhere, he was able to keep his mind on his task. In the face of much human violence and cruelty, Paramartha succeeded in producing some of the gentlest and most beautiful translations of Buddhist literature ever made into Chinese. His translation of the *Awakening of Faith in the Mahayana* is a magnificent example of the triumph of spirit over adversity, for not only is this work an accurate and useful translation, it is also a beautiful one.

Paramartha succeeded where few before him had because he remained constant in his purpose and did not allow worldly trials to defeat him. How many of us could survive such hardships, let alone produce a great translation in the midst of them? Though he is remembered for the work he did while in China, Paramartha's most arduous work surely was done before he went to China. During his years in India he must have spent long periods of time in deep and honest introspection, for where else could he have discovered the inner resources that allowed him to be at once so sensitive and strong, so determined and receptive?

While we can learn much from the examples of others, examples alone will never suffice to make us diligent. The hard work of honest introspection and change is something that each of us must do for ourselves. The secret of really gaining something from Paramartha's life story lies in realizing what it was that made him able to do so much.

Buddhist sutras generally say that we gain ten benefits by practicing diligence: we are not easily defeated by circumstances, we receive the blessings of many Buddhas, we are honored by beings in other realms, we remember the Dharma easily, we learn quickly, we become effective in our use of language, we attain deep *samadhi* states, we have fewer diseases and worries, we improve our digestion, we become enlightened more quickly.

Diligence can be likened to starting a fire by rubbing two sticks together. If we keep at it, we will heat the wood enough to cause it to burn, while if we quit too soon, we will succeed only in tiring ourselves. Nearly everything in life is like this. If we stop too soon, we will fail to reach our goal. Most people are the same—they love the strong burst of enthusiasm that first comes when a new course of action is taken, but as time goes on and things become routine, they begin to lose interest and look for something else to inspire them. Diligence is founded on knowing that deep inspiration must come from within, for when we draw on our own inner resources, there is nothing that can stop us and nothing that can make us change course too soon.

There is a Buddhist story about a pair of parrots who saw a forest fire one day. Though the flames of the fire were fearsome, the parrots decided that they still must do whatever they could to stop the blaze. Accordingly, they began carrying water in their mouths from a river nearby. Though their efforts were insufficient to extinguish the blaze, the parrots kept at their labors. Seeing how determined they were, the god of fire spoke to them saying, "Parrots, why do you bother? You can never carry enough water to put out such a huge fire."

The parrots replied, "It is our duty to try anyway. If others would help us, we might even succeed in stopping the blaze."

When the god heard their answer, he was moved by their determination and put out the fire himself. This little story illustrates a deep principle: when we are really determined to do something, powerful forces often will come to our aid. Diligence can unleash strengths in us that we never knew we had.

The *Sutra in Forty-two Sections* says that there are three important stages in learning to be diligent: the protected stage, the stage of learning good methods, and the stage of actively working for the liberation of others. The protected stage corresponds to that period of time when we are first learning how to be diligent. During this stage we have to be careful about how we approach our task because our determination alone may not be strong enough to withstand all that we will have to bear. In this stage, we must appraise ourselves honestly as we clearly assess the difficulties that lie before us. Once we have understood what will be required of us, then we must shield ourselves from those things that might cause us to fail. For example, a student who is just beginning college must learn to avoid the use of drugs because if he does not, his grades will suffer and he may lose his way. A beginning teacher must be prepared to face the disappointment of not being able to help every student he teaches, for if he is not, he may become discouraged and quit teaching altogether. When people are not prepared to shield themselves from disappointment and temptation, they too often lose heart and accomplish nothing at all. They may begin with great determination, but if they do not protect themselves properly, they may end up accomplishing nothing.

The second stage of diligence is the stage of learning good methods. Once we have learned to protect our resolve, we will begin to see more clearly the many methods that we can use to succeed at our chosen task. Once we are aware of the negative forces that we must avoid, we are free to learn the positive methods that will help us move forward. The shielded stage guards us from disappointment and negativity, while the learning stage allows us to acquire the skills that will help us accomplish our goals. For example, if a beginning college student is successful in resisting drug use, then he will be free to apply all of his energies to his studies. Similarly, if a beginning teacher is prepared for the inevitable disappointments that come with teaching, he will be in a better frame of mind to learn new methods that may produce better results.

The third stage of diligence is the stage of working for the liberation of others. While all of us would like to propel ourselves quickly to this stage, it is not possible to do so without going through the first two stages. Remember, even the Buddha had to learn how to help others. No one is born with perfect diligence. All of us must learn to develop it at some time. The Buddha taught the three stages of developing diligence because when we try to hurry our progress we too often fail. Diligence requires both emotional determination and the thoughtful application of practical methods.

Don't wait to begin. One aspect of diligence is having a clear understanding that life is short and that we must use every opportunity to progress. Once the Buddha asked a group of disciples, "How much time do you have left to live?"

One disciple said, "We can only count on having a few more days."

The Buddha said, "No. Think some more."

Another disciple said, "We can only count on having enough time to finish our meal."

Again the Buddha said, "No. Think some more."

A third disciple said, "We can only count on a single breath."

The Buddha said, "Excellent! That is all the time we have."

When you place your attention on the moment, and on the very breath you are breathing now, can you still make excuses for laziness? Can you still find reasons to avoid doing what you know you must? Diligence is based on understanding that life is short and that we must make good use of all of the time that we have. If we do not act now, we will never succeed in "escaping the prison of this dark world."

The following story can help us understand the importance of respecting ourselves enough to want to change for the better. Once Master Fo Yin was walking with the poet Su Tung-p'o when they came upon a stone statue of Avalokiteshvara bodhisattva, known in Chinese as Kuan Yin. Master Fo Yin pressed his palms together and bowed to the statue.

Su Tung-p'o then said, "We bow to Kuan Yin because she can

help us. But if this is so, why does she hold prayer beads? If we contemplate her so that she will help us, who is she contemplating?"

Master Fo Yin replied, "This is a question you must ask yourself."

Su Tung-p'o said, "How can I answer that for myself?"

Master Fo Yin said, "Look at Kuan Yin. She is contemplating herself."

Su Tung-p'o said, "I know, but why would she contemplate herself?"

Master Fo Yin replied, "It is better to rely on yourself than to rely on others."

THE FOUR DEMONS OF THIS DARK WORLD

The main reason to study the Dharma is to learn how to break the hold of the troubles and cares that so determine the lives of ordinary people. Our troubles are based on our harmful fixations and they work against us like thieves in the night, stealing all of the peace and contentment we have gathered over the years. The Buddha said that there are eighty-four thousand kinds of delusion. In many of his talks he said that all of those kinds of delusion are based on nothing more than the three poisons of greed, anger, and ignorance. "The prison of this dark world" is nothing more than our own minds when they are filled with the three poisons.

In Buddhism the word *demon* generally means those parts of ourselves that work against our best interests. Understanding our demons can be difficult because they are very hard to see. Just when we think that we are doing everything right, a demon rises in our minds and tempts us toward excess. Just when we think that we have at last learned to control some negative trait, the world itself seems to conspire against us to draw it from us again.

In this section, the sutra employs the bold image of four demons holding us in the dark prison of this world. Its injunction to escape our cramped cell stimulates our self-respect as it inspires us to greater diligence. The four demons conjured by this image are our harmful fixations, the five skandhas, death, and wrong views. Like jailors who are reflections of ourselves, these demons confine us to a prison of our own devising. This use of strong imagery is not unusual in Buddhist literature. Death is often referred to as a demon or a soldier waiting by the door, while the five skandhas frequently are portrayed as fierce ghouls who rip tranquility and contentment from our lives, leaving us with nothing but pain.

On the night when the Buddha became enlightened, he was tempted and taunted by innumerable droves of demons who came to destroy his achievement, and haul his mind back to the interminable ordinariness of deluded life. In the *Kshitigarbha Sutra* demons are described chasing and grabbing people who have been driven onto the shores of a caustic sea where they had been floating for days. With talons and fangs the demons tear flesh from the bodies of the beached swimmers as they drive them toward even deeper reaches of hell. In many sutras, people are described as wailing and screaming as they boil in vats of oil or wander naked across freezing lands where there is no food and no relief from pain. Practitioners can make of these descriptions what they like. Some people take them literally, others see them as imaginative embellishments of our psychological fears and urges, while still others see them as artistic expansions on the notion that we are what we think we are and that all of us get exactly what we deserve. While it is surely not healthy to dwell on images as harsh as these, it is not healthy either to completely ignore the horrors they suggest. Buddhism is a comprehensive religion of the mind, and it would be a falsification of its profundity to pretend that any part of life should be hidden from our awareness or kept in secret forever. We are what we are, and when we imagine otherwise we become as demons ourselves.

Once a disciple said to Master Chao Chou (779–897), "Master, you always behave with compassion and wisdom and you seem to have attained a state of perfect virtue. May I ask you, where will you be one hundred years from now?"

Chao Chou said, "I'll be in hell!"

"What?" his disciple replied. "You are so virtuous. Why would you go to hell?"

Chao Chou said, "To save you."

THE FIFTH REALIZATION

Study Widely, Listen Carefully

Realize that ignorance gives rise to the cycle of birth and death. The bodhisattva studies widely, listens carefully, and thinks often in order to increase his wisdom and develop his talents in speaking so that he is fit to teach and transform others, and show them the greatest joy.

How can we defeat our demons if we do not know that we have any? How can we overcome our ignorance if we pretend that we are wise? The first noble truth of Buddhism states that life is unsatisfactory and that all of us must experience pain and sorrow. Who can deny this truth? Realizing that this is so is the start of wisdom. The great mistake people make is they turn away from the Dharma because they want to turn away from themselves. They do not want to see the demonic side of being. They do not want to know themselves. In their feigned perfection, their defilements, which grow like mushrooms in the dark, become only worse, for to ignore an unconscious condition of the mind is to increase it. We turn away from all that is good when we fail to account for that which is bad. This is why the Buddha counsels us to realize that "ignorance gives rise to the cycle of birth and death." In English the word ignorance is derived from the word "ignore." In Chinese ignorance literally means "without light," or "without understanding." There can be no light in places we choose to ignore, and there can be no understanding when we turn from the true nature of our human wants and fears.

A fundamental teaching of the Buddha is that the worlds we live in have been created by our own actions. Your family, your friends, your health, your needs, your nation, and everything else that you may call your own is truly your own because it was made by you. Your intentions and your karma brought it into being. The cycle of birth and death referred to in this section is the same as the prison of this dark world mentioned in the last section. Calling it a cycle now is simply a more accurate way of describing how the prison is built, and how it is filled again and again with the same beings whose endemic recidivism is the only cause of their confinement.

In the last section, the Buddha introduced the idea that we are imprisoned by the four demons of our mental defilements, the five skandhas, death, and wrong views. It is important to understand what these demons are and what they mean to us if we truly hope to overcome the ignorance that gives rise to the cycle of birth and death and to escape from the prison of this dark world.

The demon of our mental defilements is everything within us that works to harm us or to harm others. This demon is especially vicious when we ignore it, or pretend that its urges are something other than what they are. The demon of our five skandhas is everything that allows us to believe that our individual awareness should be preeminent and above others. The face of this demon is everything that we vainly believe to be unique and important about ourselves. The demon of death is the brevity of any particular incarnation or the false appearance that it is hopeless to try to change. The demon of wrong views is the demon of misunderstanding the Buddha's message. This is the demon that cajoles us to dismiss what we have not understood, or to turn away from that which does not flatter us. If we hope to disentangle ourselves from the cycle of birth and death, we must escape from the prison of ignorance that is guarded by these four powerful demons. This is why "the bodhisattva studies widely, listens carefully, and thinks often" about the Dharma. The Buddha's central lessons cannot be learned in a day, or in a year, or even in a lifetime. They are not something to be noted and forgotten; they are guides that must be consulted at all times.

Once there was a man who felt that he had been insulted by someone. He wanted to get even with the person who had offended him, but he could not think how. He held his hatred in his heart and walked around feeling bitter and angry. One day a sorcerer asked him why he was so bitter. The man explained that he had been insulted and that he could not think of a good way to get even. The sorcerer said, "I know of a way to get even."

The man said, "Please tell me what it is."

The sorcerer said, "I know a curse that will kill the man you hate. However, I doubt that you will want to use it because one of the conditions of the curse is that if you use it, you will have to die too."

The man said, "I don't care! Tell me what it is!"

The sorcerer told him the curse and a few days later he

learned that the man had died. All anger is like this. It always turns against us and harms us the most. Our minds control the ways that we react to the conditions of our lives. Ignorant behavior, as in the story above, arises in a mind that is dark and unaware of the depth of life.

Let us contrast the previous story with another. Master Ryokan lived very simply in a rude forest hut. One evening he returned from preaching the Dharma only to find that a thief was looking inside his hut.

Ryokan said, "You won't find anything in there. All I have are the clothes on my back." With that he took his clothes off and handed them to the thief. "Here take these," he said.

The thief clutched the clothing to his chest and ran away. As he disappeared into the night, Ryokan gazed toward the moon that shone down on his naked body. "How sad," he sighed, "that I cannot give him this beautiful moon as well."

Ignorance is that which causes us to be trapped in the cycle of birth and death. When we understand this cycle and our own parts in keeping it going, we will understand how to escape it. Buddhism is a religion that is made up of equal parts of wisdom and morality. Wisdom can be thought of as all that we know and understand about life, while morality can be thought of as the way that we behave, especially when our behavior affects the lives of others. Buddhist wisdom is different from what most of us think of as learning or intellectual achievement, for the wisdom that the Buddha taught is always concerned with life and the many ways that we can benefit the beings living around us. The modern world presents us with many examples of "wisdom" that has caused more harm than good. People are capable of discovering marvelous inventions, but when these inventions are used to harm others their implementation cannot be called wise by any stretch of the imagination. True wisdom is deep insight into the nature of being. It is profound understanding of motive and intention. Wisdom is that which guides us to benefit both ourselves and others at the same time. It is that which leads us from the delusive cycle of birth and death.

In addition to the basic kinds of ignorance we have already discussed—greed, anger, pride, and doubt—the Buddha also talked about several erroneous beliefs that frequently bind us to self-perpetuating cycles of harm and ignorance. These beliefs are particularly difficult to overcome because, though they are fallacious, they are founded on rational thinking processes.

The first erroneous belief is the belief that one's body is something that one actually possesses, and that this possession is something that must be clung to with all one's might. Even a cursory acquaintance with modern biology should lead us to understand that our bodies are composed of materials that we cannot control and that they are regulated by systems that we do not understand. How can we possibly hope to cling to this mysterious mélange of mysterious parts? It is not irrational to form the thought of wanting to cling to the body, but it becomes irrational to persist in this thought in the face of so much evidence against its possibility.

The second erroneous belief has two sides to it. On one side is the belief that life ends completely at death, while on the other side is the belief that an immortal soul continues to live after death. The Buddha said that both of these beliefs are wrong. Life does not end with the death of the physical body, but neither does some soul that now inhabits the body continue to live as if without interruption, in a disembodied state that must be immortal since it no longer is physical. The Buddha taught that when the body perishes, the karma that was generated by it continues on in a sort of "mind stream" that eventually gives rise to another life. This continuation is the essence of the cycle of birth and death.

The third erroneous belief is the belief that the four noble truths are false, or that the world does not operate on a cause-and-effect basis. This belief all too often leads people to think that their actions do not have karmic effects and that it does not matter what they do or do not do. This belief can be very dangerous if it is entertained by someone with violent or antisocial tendencies.

The fourth erroneous belief is any belief that keeps one from understanding the Dharma. Any lesser belief that clouds the mind or prevents higher learning is a serious impediment to continuing growth and development. Beliefs of this sort might be such ideas as dialectical materialism, fatalism, nihilism, misunderstanding the principles of science, and so on.

The fifth erroneous belief is the belief in any religious practice that does not work. Fasting in order to gain psychic powers or committing suicide in order to go to heaven are examples of this.

Ignorance of the true nature of things can lead us to make many mistakes. The following story can be interpreted in many ways. Once three Buddhist monks were traveling together along the banks of a slow-moving stream. In the distance they could see a small village. The monks decided to go to the village to beg for alms. Just as they made their decision, one of them noticed a head of cabbage floating down the stream. He said, "We had better not go to that village up there. Look how wasteful the villagers are. Someone has tossed a whole head of cabbage into the stream."

The other monks agreed. "There is no reason to preach the Dharma to people like that," they said.

Just then, a woman came running down the path toward them. "Masters," she cried, "Have you seen a cabbage floating in the stream? It fell out of my hands just a few minutes ago! It would be such a waste to lose it!"

With that the monks all looked at each other and said, "We had better go there after all."

Sometimes the smallest details can make the biggest difference. Buddhist sutras generally describe ignorance as being a sort of darkness, but sometimes ignorance is nothing more than a small misunderstanding, or a small misinterpretation of the facts. The monks in the story above might have wandered for a long time before they found another village as good as the one they almost passed by.

LISTENING, SPEAKING

Master T'ai Hsu (1899–1947) once said, "The wisdom we gain from listening to the truth establishes our faith. The wisdom we gain from thinking about the truth establishes our morality. The wisdom we gain from practicing the truth establishes our relationship with the Buddha."

Master T'ai Hsu placed his statements in that order because to overcome ignorance we must first hear the truth. Having heard the truth, we must think about it. Having thought about it, we must practice it. This basic order is one that should be followed again and again as new aspects of the Dharma become clear to us. First we hear a new idea, then we think about it, then we apply it to our lives. If we fail to follow any of these steps, we will find it difficult to progress because our nascent wisdom will be weak in one of these important areas. Though this point is obvious, I rarely see people applying it as they should.

If we are to study widely and learn as much as we can about the Buddha's teaching, it follows that we must be open-minded. Close-mindedness or narrow, sectarian thinking can only be a hindrance to real growth. Sometimes when people first begin to study Buddhism, they latch on to one small part of its vast tradition and refuse to consider that there can be other points of view, or that the truth can be seen from more than one angle. People like that often throw themselves into meditation or into one kind of Buddhist practice without recognizing that there are many ways to become enlightened. The Buddha never said to be close-minded or intolerant of practices that we do not understand!

In truth, it is very difficult to say exactly what the right way to practice Buddhism is; there are so many possibilities that we must be sure to keep our minds open to all of them, even as we focus on those aspects of the Dharma that we have chosen to perfect. Generally speaking, all Buddhist studies should be guided by the three trainings—morality, meditation, and wisdom. The three trainings were described by the Buddha as a basic way to approach the Dharma, irrespective of what our personal inclinations may or may not be. The three trainings tell us first to build a moral foundation, then to perfect our meditation and introspection, and lastly to become wise through these first two activities. Whether we are esoteric, or Theravada, or Ch'an, or Pure Land practitioners, all of us should rely on the three trainings as basic guidelines for our practice. Beyond that, we have the freedom to choose which sutras or which techniques we may want to study. We also have the freedom to choose those teachers whom we feel will benefit us the most. In choosing one way over another, however, we should never allow ourselves to lose respect for other people who may have made decisions that are different from our own.

The *Shurangama Sutra* describes the exquisite listening ability of Avalokiteshvara, whose name means "he who listens to the sound of the world." His listening ability is described as having three wonderful aspects: it is able to penetrate the truth, contain the truth, and remember the truth. Penetrating the truth means that his power to listen and understand cannot be blocked by anything. Unlike eyesight, which may be blocked by a wall, his listening abilities cannot be hindered by anything. Containing the truth means that his listening abilities are not confined to only one angle at a time. Unlike eyesight which can only see one side of a thing at a time, Avalokiteshvara can hear everything in all directions at once, and thus he "contains" them all. Remembering the truth means that what he heard in the past, he still remembers today. Our hearing may penetrate anything and contain everything, but if we do not remember, it will be as if we had heard nothing at all. All Buddhists should model themselves on Avalokiteshvara as much as possible. There is nothing anywhere that we should not seek to learn and understand.

When we have succeeded in acquiring listening abilities like Avalokiteshvara, we will be ready to begin to develop our talents in speaking so that we are fit to teach and transform others, and show them the greatest joy. Eventually our speaking abilities should be as unblocked as our listening abilities, for only when we understand how to express ourselves will we be able to help others learn to see the truth. This kind of speaking ability should not be confused with the ability to argue or debate, for the purpose of this skill is only to lead people toward the truth, not to defeat them or win anything from them. This kind of skill is acquired by first listening to others and understanding their hopes and fears, then slowly learning how to respond to them in such a way that our words can be a help to them. Ultimately, we would hope that our words will "transform them" by leading them to a deeper understanding of the teachings of the Buddha. Remember, ultimately all knowledge is self-knowledge, so we should never expect our words to be much more than guides for others as we pass through the conditions of this realm.

Talking too much is another habit that should be avoided when trying to learn the skill of transforming others with our words. Deep transformation is always an intensely personal inner process. In most cases, we will bring more benefit by listening to others than by talking to them. A few well-placed words will always be more valuable than hours of babbling. Once the great philosopher Socrates was enrolling students in an informal class he was giving on public speaking. The fee for the class was ten cents. A young man came to register for the class, and as he was doing so he explained at great length why he wanted to learn to become a good speaker, what the value of speaking was, and so on. After he at last stopped speaking, Socrates asked him to pay an additional ten cents. The student was shocked to hear this and asked him why he was being required to pay twice as much as the other people in the class.

Socrates said, "The other students are paying ten cents to learn how to talk, but you must pay twenty cents because not only do I have to teach you how to talk, I also must teach you how to stop talking."

Buddhist sutras generally mention four important aspects of good speaking. Though these aspects are ideals that are beyond the reach of most of us most of the time, they still are very good indications of what the Buddha meant when he said that we should develop our talents in speaking so that we will be fit to teach and transform others, and show them the greatest joy.

The first aspect is called "unblocked understanding of the Dharma." *Unblocked* means that there is nothing preventing us from seeing and knowing what is denoted by the words of the Buddha. If our speaking talents are based on an unblocked understanding of the Buddha's words, we will be able to know how to answer any question that is put to us. The second aspect is called "unblocked understanding of the principles underlying the Dharma." It is one thing to know what the words mean, but it is another thing to understand the deep principles upon which they are based. The third aspect is called "unblocked expression of the Dharma." This means that we are able to express the truths of the Dharma in terms that are well suited to our audience. The fourth aspect is called "unblocked joy in teaching the Dharma." We may possess the first three aspects, but if we lack the fourth, few people will benefit from our talents.

The important thing to remember about developing your speaking talents is that these talents are not something that should be used to lord over others, defeat them in verbal debates, or bore them with endless droning. Deep and effective speaking abilities rely as much on silence and listening as they do on actual speech.

The *Sutra of Vimalakirti's Dicsourse* contains a famous passage that illustrates this idea very well. Once a large group of very advanced disciples of the Buddha went to visit Vimalakirti. The subject of going "beyond duality" arose, and the group discussed it from many different angles. When someone asked Manjushri what his thoughts were, Manjushri said, "In my view, going beyond duality means going beyond all phenomenal appearances, beyond all questions and answers, beyond all words, all speech, and all analytical thought processes."

When he was finished speaking, Manjushri asked Vimalakirti what he thought. Vimalakirti looked at him and said nothing.

Without using a single word, Vimalakirti revealed that of all the learned people who were present, his speaking abilities were paramount, for when we truly go beyond duality, we also go beyond all words and all descriptions.

In contrast, but not in contradiction, to this story from the *Sutra of Vimalakirti's Discourse*, there is the story of Master Chih Yi (538–97), who once spoke for three whole months on the first word of the Chinese title of the *Lotus Sutra*. The word he spoke about can be translated as "wondrous," but the significance of his talking for so long is not contained in the word itself; the point is that all of the Dharma can be accessed from any aspect or part of it. Great speakers simply know when to speak at length and when to remain silent. Sometimes a long lecture is just the thing, and sometimes a smile is all that is needed. The main reason to develop speaking abilities is to help others and lead them to the "greatest joy" of understanding the truth for themselves.

The *Sutra in Forty-two Sections* says, "One who sees the way is like someone who has brought a torch into a dark room—suddenly the darkness is gone and all that remains is light. If we study the way and see the truth, our ignorance will disappear and light will appear everywhere." More than anything else, Buddhism is a religion of wisdom, the wisdom that arises when we see ourselves as we really are.

THE SIXTH REALIZATION

The Importance of Being Generous

Realize that resenting poverty and suffering leads only to more of the same. A bodhisattva is generous and equal minded toward both friend and foe. He does not dwell on old wrongs, or make new enemies.

This realization concerns our attitudes toward poverty and wealth. There are two basic things to understand about the meaning of this realization. The first is that neither poverty nor wealth are permanent states of being; sometimes poor people become wealthy and sometimes wealthy people lose everything they have. No material condition is permanent. The second important thing to understand about this realization is that the dualistic pair—poverty and wealth—can have many different meanings. The Buddha is not just talking about material poverty and wealth, but also about intellectual, moral, and spiritual poverty and wealth. All of us surely have known someone who was spiritually wealthy though materially poor. And most have probably also seen the opposite of this kind of person—someone who is materially very wealthy, but spiritually mean and angry. Karmic fruits should never be understood in terms of a debased equation wherein the quantity of one's material possessions is believed to indicate the degree of one's virtue. Material wealth and spiritual wealth are not produced by the same conditions or the same energies.

The sutra says that "resenting poverty and suffering leads only to more of the same." This is so because when we are resentful, we tend to blame others for our suffering, while ignoring its deeper causes. Poor people who resent the wealthy would do much better if they used their energies to create conditions that were not so disagreeable. Wealthy people who resent poor people or who hold society in contempt are only planting the seeds of their eventual downfall. All of us must learn to live together and help each other during the brief period of time that we inhabit this realm.

Resentment is a low emotion caused by dwelling on the negative features of a situation without doing anything about them. People who are resentful usually blame others for problems that are really their own. There are four basic kinds of resentment mentioned in Buddhist sutras. The first is resenting the heavens for one's "fate." This sort of resentment frequently leads people to adopt perverse religious views in order to change their fates, or to appease the gods that they believe are persecuting them. The second kind of resentment is directed toward the social system or the environment. People blame the economic system, the political system, the climate, or the land for their problems. The third is resenting one's family or taking one's resentments out on family members. A great deal of domestic violence and abuse is caused when people blame their loved ones for conditions that are beyond their control.

The fourth is resenting our friends for not helping us when we should be helping ourselves.

The *Path of Practice Sutra* says, "Those who want to improve themselves should realize that when they turn their anger on others, they are hurting themselves most of all. They are like sticks of wood using fire to attack others; in the end they burn themselves the most." The *Sutra on the Samadhi of Great Merit* says, "Rid yourself of passion and hate, and do not let yourself be resentful or mean. Practice compassion and look upon your enemies as your friends."

Nowhere has it been said that we should not recognize social or political problems when they exist, or that we should not strive to make the best of a poor environment. The deep meaning of this realization is not that we should passively accept everything that happens to us, but that we should work to change bad conditions through acts of kindness and generosity, and that we should not allow ourselves to become angry or resentful while doing so. Resentment is an inner state that we have the power to control. It is a sign of ignorance and "harmful fixation." If we feel that we are susceptible to feelings of resentment, we should strive to monitor our moods and behavior. The moment we find ourselves feeling resentful, we should stop and reflect on what is causing our mood and why we are choosing to indulge in this negative state.

The single best cure for all mental and emotional defilements is to emphasize their positive opposites. At first this sort of emphasis can feel contrived and unsatisfying, but in time we will see that it produces very good results, for it is based on the deep principles that underlie all of our mental functions. The mind works in dualistic pairs: anger is the polar opposite of love or kindness, passion is the opposite of reason, fear is the opposite of trust. When we fall under the spell of any emotional state, we must look to balance it by bringing forth its opposite. If we find ourselves indulging in resentment, we must try to be as reasonable and compassionate as we can. At first, this behavior may feel strained, but in a very short time it will lead us to a much healthier state of mind. If we are honest with ourselves, we will soon conclude that our resentment was nothing more than a harmful fixation on a false appearance and that persisting in it would not have brought any good results at all. Indeed, an ongoing cycle of resentment and anger can lead to violent explosions that are far out of proportion to the imaginary "offenses" that started them in the first place. Daily, there are stories in the paper about these kinds of violent eruptions. As we shake our heads in wonder at them, we should also remember that nearly all of them began as a small irritation that someone allowed to grow into a boil of resentment, and from there into an angry criminal act. Is it any wonder that the Buddha called such moods demonic? Or that Buddhist art for centuries has depicted grotesque demons as a warning to our subconscious, as well as to our conscience? As long as we are alive, none of us should dare to stop monitoring our moods and feelings for signs of resentment or anger. Harmful fixations are generally not dangerous if we identify them in time and take proper measures to eradicate them. When we fail to notice them, or when we lie to ourselves about their true natures, however, they can grow very quickly into horrendous monsters that have the capacity to ruin all the good that we have ever done.

The following tale reminds us that only wisdom can overcome ignorance, and that it is impossible run away from ourselves. Once there was a sage who agreed to teach three young students the way to enlightenment. Fearing that they might be lured from the path by the glitter of the world, the sage took his students to a place deep in the mountains, where he taught them for many years. When the boys reached the age of sixteen, the sage decided that it was time to take them into a city to show them what life in the world was really like. No sooner did they enter the city than the sage noticed that his students were fascinated by the beautiful women that were walking about there. To keep their minds on the truth, the sage said, "Be careful of them for they are not what they seem. They are man-eating tigers!"

They continued touring the city. They visited temples and shrines, and called on several renowned masters. At nightfall the sage led them back to the mountains. When they were safe in their retreat once again, he asked, "What did you learn today? What was the most interesting thing you saw?"

Without hesitation the three replied in unison, "The man-eating tigers!"

We cannot run from who we are. That sage would have done better to raise the boys in a town where they would have learned to understand themselves from an early age. We must learn to disentangle ourselves from the fixations of our minds, not to run from them or pretend that they can be ignored.

This sixth realization counsels us to be "generous and equal minded toward both friend and foe." Equal mindedness is the balance point at the center of the mind's constellations of dualistic emotions. When first glimpsed, this point may seem very small, but after we have visited it often, we will realize that it actually contains all of the universe. Equal mindedness is the goal of Buddhist morality, the basis of Buddhist meditation, and the fruit of Buddhist wisdom. It is the portal to Buddha mind, the essence of enlightenment, and the fulfillment of all that we are. Buddhism is often called "the middle path" because of the great rewards that can be gained by equal mindedness. When we are equal minded we do not see a distinction between friend and foe, we do not notice resentment, and we do not feel selfish. Deep equal mindedness is a positive state that rests in the knowledge that all beings are one and that generosity is the only natural state of the heart.

The *Sutra on the Three Dharmas of Great Wisdom* says, "If you want to become enlightened, be equal minded among all sentient beings." The *Moon Lamp Samadhi Sutra* says, "To be equal minded among all things means that there is no sense of this or that, or of discriminating or not discriminating, or of doing something, or of giving rise to something, or of creating something, or of extinguishing something. All delusion, all analytical thought, and all ideas are simply stopped."

GENEROSITY

Generosity is a very important virtue. Coupled with patience, it is basic to all social activity. Generosity is that virtue which reaches out to others, while patience is that which allows us to tolerate the unkindness with which we may be met. The Buddha said that the six most important virtues of a bodhisattva are generosity, restraint, patience under insult, diligence, concentration, and wisdom.

Once during the time of the Buddha there was a woman who was very poor. She went to Katyayana and explained her plight and asked him what she should do. Katyayana said that she should stop worrying because he knew of a way to change her situation. The woman begged him to tell her what it was.

Katyayana said, "Sell your poverty to others!"

"Sell it?" the woman asked. "If people bought poverty, why soon there would be no poverty in the world! And who would want to buy someone else's poverty anyway?"

Katyayana said, "Sell it to me."

The woman said, "I don't know how to sell it. What should I do?"

Katyayana said, "All you have to do is be generous to everyone. That is the way to sell poverty.

"You see," he continued, "in your last life you were never generous with anyone. You hoarded everything and never gave anything to anyone. So now you are poor. If you can learn to be generous, you will see that your situation will quickly change."

When he was finished speaking, the woman realized that Katyayana had indeed told her the truth. In just a few moments she had learned how to eradicate her poverty, as well as how to be a good bodhisattva, which is far more important.

This realization says "a bodhisattva is generous and equal minded toward both friend and foe." Some might wonder how a poor woman is supposed to be generous. Isn't generosity something that only rich people can practice? The answer to this question is no. Generosity is a deep state of mind that is based on the recognition that the well being of others is fully as important as our own. There are many ways to practice generosity, not just one. We can be generous with our time, with our wisdom, with our skills, with our willingness to listen to others, with encouragement, and so on. Material generosity is important, and no Buddhist temple would ever have been built without it, but this is not the only way to give.

Buddhist sutras generally recognize three important kinds of generosity: material generosity, emotional generosity, and the generosity of helping others learn the Dharma. Each of these forms of generosity is two-sided. On the one side our generosity helps others, while on the other side it helps us. Properly practiced, generosity teaches us to be compassionate toward others, large minded in our view of the world, and unattached to our own possessions or points of view. Though material generosity begins on the material plane, it almost always rises above that. Gifts of money or goods show others that we care about them and want them to be happy. Material gifts to schools and temples help others benefit from the Dharma, while donations to Buddhist organizations help fund the work of translating Buddhist literature and educating the next generation of Buddhist practitioners.

Emotional generosity means giving of ourselves. The Buddha described this form of generosity as teaching others not to be afraid. Fear is the great unrecognized emotion. It leads us to selfishness, anger, resentment, cowardice, and many other negative states of mind. The Buddha taught the Dharma to help us learn to stop being afraid. Once we understand the conditions of life, we will no longer fear them, for we will know how to use them to our advantage.

The greatest kind of generosity is teaching others the Dharma, for only the Dharma can show them how to free themselves from all forms of suffering. Though this is the greatest kind of generosity, it should be recognized that Dharma generosity cannot really be separated from material or emotional generosity. In the best cases, the three kinds of generosity are simply three parts of the same act. For example, when we enter a temple, we receive the gift of the material generosity of the donors who built the temple. When we experience the tranquility of the Buddha Hall, we receive the gift of their emotional generosity. And when we learn something of the Dharma inside the temple, we receive their gift of the truth. The people that built that temple for our use gave us a gift that will touch every part of our being if we are receptive to it and willing to receive it.

The fourth kind of generosity is receiving the gifts of others. Most of us think that we can only be generous when we give something to someone, but we can also be generous when we receive, for when we receive we allow another person to give and we allow them to establish a bond with us that did not exist before. The next time that you feel that it would be easier to refuse something that someone has offered you, ask yourself if your refusal is truly the most generous thing that you could do. You will almost certainly see that it is not. Very often it is easier to give than to receive, and for just this reason we should strive to be gracious and grateful receivers of others' kindness fully as much as we should strive to give something to them.

At its deepest level a perfect act of generosity dwells in conscious emptiness, in the awareness that each of the three components of the act of giving is without absolute substance. This means that one is aware in a very deep sense that there is no giver, no gift, and no recipient of any gift. This level of awareness is not the same as merely thinking that nothing is happening, for the spiritual energy that inspires the giver to include the recipient in a selfless act is very real. Indeed, this spiritual energy is a manifest aspect of the omniscient Buddha mind that underlies all conscious acts. The profound compassion that leads to acts of deep generosity is an aspect of the Buddha that dwells within us. A glimpse of this compassion is an intimation of the depth of awareness that is our true potential, and the true nature of our beings. In this sense, compassion and generosity can be understood as windows through which we view the Buddha himself. Ultimately, this view will lead to a state of being in which the viewer is absorbed into the view, in which the deluded self is led to understand that the real basis of its being is immensely greater than anything it had ever been able to conceive on its own. To become a Buddha, we must surrender our lower self to the full

expanse of higher awareness. To become a Buddha we must
allow ourselves to be enveloped by that awareness. To say that
individual awareness is a false appearance dependent on harmful
fixations is to say that our conceptions of selfhood are limited to
one end of a vast spectrum that grades seamlessly from the
"awareness" of a one-celled animal to that of an omniscient
Buddha. Shakyamuni Buddha taught the importance of compassion and generosity for their intrinsic value, but also because
experiencing these states is the surest means of all to experience
the Buddha who is the one truth and the knower of all.

DO NOT DWELL ON OLD WRONGS

Not dwelling on old wrongs is also a form of generosity, as well as
wisdom, for when we dwell on negative memories we often become
resentful or angry, and these states just lead toward more of the
same. The cycle of birth and death can be seen in the large picture
of one lifetime after another, but it can also be seen in the details
of one life. Dwelling on old wrongs eventually leads to new wrongs,
which then quickly become old wrongs in someone else's mind.
Returning anger with anger, seeking revenge, brooding about the
past, refusing to forgive—all of these are actions that perpetuate
the cycle of suffering and pain. Most evil is caused by people react-
ing negatively to the perception that someone has done them
wrong. The way to stop this cycle is to take responsibility for your
part in it. As much as you can, forgive and forget, and do not dwell
on the people that you believe have harmed you. Not only will you
benefit, but so will society in general. *Spreading the Light* says,
"Repay anger with kindness; never dwell on old wrongs."

During the time of the Buddha, Devadatta tried to harm the
Buddha several times—by telling lies about him, by attacking him

with a drunken elephant, and by shoving a boulder down a hill at him. To none of this did the Buddha ever once respond with anger or resentment. Instead, he said, "Devadatta is only helping me by urging me forward. He is my great teacher." If you can see your "foes" who have done wrong to you as your "great teachers," you will have understood this realization and more, for forgiveness of this magnitude is always followed by an enormous upsurge in joy and good fortune. When we break the chains of the past like this, we actually change the conditions and direction of our karma.

While most of us realize that it is best not to "dwell on old wrongs," few of us are able to do this. The right way to let go of the past is to benefit from it. Rather than resent something that we perceive as a "wrong," we should look at it more closely and discover how it may help us. No one grows spiritually who experiences nothing. Setbacks and hardships can and should be used to train us and spur us on to new achievements. Countries that have only one political party stagnate, while those that have functioning democratic institutions do not. Bodies that never get any exercise become weak, while those that are forced to strain themselves grow strong and healthy. Hardship is nothing more than our perception of one side of a dualistic pair. Whenever we find ourselves being challenged by hardship, we should consider how it strengthens us and helps us. When others insult us, or complain about us, or treat us badly, we should accept them as teachers who can help us become stronger and wiser. "Old wrongs" are nothing more than old lessons that we have not yet fully learned. To resent them is to compound the problem that brought them on in the first place.

The following story shows how important our attitudes can be. Once there was a man who was very curious about the difference between heaven and hell. He knew that beings in heaven were very happy and that those in hell were very unhappy. One day, he met sage who told him that he could take him to both heaven and hell so that he could see for himself what the differences between them were. The man said that he was ready to go immediately.

Suddenly, the sage transported them to hell. The man was surprised at first because the scene before him was very similar to a scene on earth. A group of people were seated at a table eating dinner. When he looked more closely, however, he saw that the people were using chopsticks that were three feet long. Since the chopsticks were so long, the people at the table kept bumping each other and dropping their food. No one was getting enough to eat and everyone was very irritable and nasty.

Suddenly the scene changed, and the man knew that he was in heaven. But once again he was surprised at what he saw. Before him there was a group of people not all that different from the group he had seen in hell. This group, too, was seated at a table eating dinner, and they, too, were using chopsticks that were three feet long. When the man looked more closely, however, he saw that instead of dropping their food and becoming irritable as the beings in hell had been doing, the heavenly beings were using their long chopsticks to feed each other. Everyone was laughing and smiling and they were all getting plenty to eat.

THE SEVENTH REALIZATION

Morality Fosters Self-control

Realize that the five desires bring nothing but trouble. Though we live in this world, we do not become stained by worldly pleasures. Instead, we think often of a monk's garb, his bowl, and his chanting instruments. Having set our minds on monastic life, we uphold the way and purify ourselves. Our morality encompasses all, our compassion includes everyone.

In the second realization, the Buddha explained that "excessive desire causes suffering," and that the way to overcome this problem is to "have few desires… and you will be content in body and mind." He also says that "the cycle of birth and death arises from greed and desire." In this seventh realization, the topic again is desire, but the focus of the Buddha's comments is slightly different. Morality is now the means to overcome the "five desires." Since basic Buddhist morality is concerned mainly with restraint, the shift in focus between these two realizations may not be as great as it first seems.

This realization can be thought of as a more detailed explanation of how to control excessive desire.

Most people believe that morality confines them while the five desires set them free. We shall see in a moment why this is not true.

Roughly speaking the five desires are the desire for wealth, sex, fame, food, and sleep. In a more philosophical context, they can also be understood to be any sensual craving associated with seeing, hearing, smelling, tasting, or touching. However we define them, the five desires of this realization are material desires that are wholly "of this world." This is why the Buddha also says "though we live in this world, we do not become stained by worldly pleasures." The way to enlightenment requires dedication to the beings of this world, but not to the incidental sensual pleasures that may arise from this dedication. It is easy for a bodhisattva to fail in this area because as his concern for others grows, his ability to attract people to him also grows. Though the *Sutra of the Eight Realizations of Great Beings* is aimed at lay disciples, the Buddha evokes the image of a monk in this realization to remind us of how we should think about our place in the world. While outwardly we may resemble ordinary people, inwardly we should think of ourselves as monks who have renounced the five desires and all of the worldly pleasures that are associated with them. As "our compassion includes everyone" our morality must also "encompass all."

The five desires are seductive. That is why we need philosophies and moral rules to help us avoid becoming entangled in them. Worldly cravings are characterized by the way they draw us in and then trap us in a complex tangle of unpleasant options and disagreeable outcomes. Who has not experienced this kind of trouble? The first noble truth says that life is unsatisfactory or that it is marked by inevitable suffering. The five desires are those energies that draw us only deeper into this level of reality. You may deny the first noble truth when you believe that it is convenient for you to do so, but your denial one day will be seen for what it really was—a convenience that allowed you to indulge in something you would have been better off leaving alone. The older we get, the more self-evident this truth becomes. Most of us discover the depths of the first noble truth through a mixture of hearing about it and experiencing it for ourselves. Only after we are convinced of its validity will we be ready to learn the second noble truth—the origin of suffering.

The origin of all suffering can be found among the "three poisons" of greed, anger, and ignorance. The five desires are a more detailed description of greed. Greed, anger, and ignorance are called the three poisons because they kill spiritual joy and ruin goodness. Sometimes they are also called the "three fires" because they consume our joy if we let them.

The five desires draw us in by a kind of selective hypnosis that emphasizes certain details of our cravings while ignoring others. If we crave wealth, we see only what we can buy, how others will be impressed with us, or how we will be able to avoid life's inconveniences. We do not see how we will become cold or arrogant, how we will isolate ourselves from others, or how we will ultimately become dull because we have ceased to have experiences that deepen us. When we emphasize excitement, we fail to see the sorrow that trails just behind. When we emphasize pride, we fail to see the shame we cause. When we emphasize power, we fail to see the misery that must ensue from its inevitable misuses.

If we crave sex, we tend to emphasize the beauty of the person we desire, the loneliness we feel without them, and the joy that we will feel when we are with them. When passion rises in the breast, who thinks of the day when it must cool? And yet, the wise know that there is a difference between mere sexual desire and the deep love that signifies a profound spiritual bond. The desire for fame is an exaggeration of the normal wish for social acceptance and to be well thought of. Ironically, this exaggeration contradicts itself, for fame all too often is acquired by harming the very people we would like to have approve of us.

Generally speaking, each of the five desires can be understood as an exaggeration of a normal and valuable human need. The desire for wealth is an exaggeration of the normal desire to have a safe home and an adequate income. The desire for sex is an exaggeration of the normal urge to have a loving partner and a family. Overeating is an exaggeration of the normal desire to nourish the body, while excessive sleeping or laziness (in the absence of disease) is an exaggeration of a normal need to rest.

When we gaze upon our needs with a balanced sense of wisdom, we will be far less likely to be seduced by any one of them. Most of us have control of at least some of our basic human urges. If we can apply the reasoning that gives us control over these urges to all of the five desires, we will go a long way toward discovering the equal mindedness of the Buddha's middle path. Desire is not wrong if it is kept in proportion. When it is allowed to grow into a fire or transform into a poison, however, it will always lead to suffering.

The *Flower Garland Sutra* says, "Sentient beings pass through the long night of their many lives dreaming of the five desires, following the five desires, greedily clinging to the five desires. Their minds are set on them and so they continuously indulge in weakness and remain trapped in the cycle of birth and death." The *Sutra of Fathers and Sons* says, "As soon as we understand the problems caused by the five desires, we will want to disentangle ourselves from them. Nothing in the world is greater than wisdom that cleanses the mind of desire."

Just as greed can be further analyzed into the five desires, so the troubles caused by these desires can be further analyzed into five basic types. The first trouble is an increase in conflict. When we indulge in any of the five desires, we tend to have more conflicts with the people around us. The second trouble is an increased sense of nervousness or anxiety. The five desires strain our normal capacities to the point where we begin to feel unsettled and ill at ease no matter where we are or what we are doing. The third trouble is a tendency to harm others. As desire pulls us deeper into its delusional realm, we run the risk of harming others to gain more for ourselves. The fourth is we become unrealistic. As desire increases, our thinking tends to become fantastic or impractical; we lose the sense of well-grounded reason that is so important to the spiritual path. The fifth is we become inconsistent and flighty. A desire that has been thwarted here leads us to seek there for its elusive reflection in yet some other impossible scheme. We run from one thing to the next in pursuit of something that does not even exist.

Desire is like honey on the blade of a knife. If we are careful about sampling it and if we know that the sharp edge is there, we will probably not harm ourselves. But if we are ignorant of its true nature, we will surely cut ourselves on the steel that lies concealed beneath the sweetness. This is why the Buddha counsels us to keep the image of a monk in our minds. As we live in the world, we must be careful to control what we hope to gain for ourselves, for if we allow ourselves to slide into a life of greed and craving, there is no guarantee that we will be able to free ourselves from it soon. Desire is like a fire, for it can burn all that we have worked for and saved through the years.

The best way to deal with desires and prevent them from becoming excessive is to frequently take stock of ourselves in the light of the five precepts. The five precepts are no killing, no stealing, no lying, no sexual misconduct, and no irresponsible use of drugs or alcohol. If we find that we are beginning to violate any of these basic precepts, we must conclude that one or more of the five desires is beginning to take root in our life. The moment we discover this, we should begin to use the four contemplations discussed in the chapter on the first realization. These contemplations were designed by the Buddha to help us gain mental control over the kinds of problems created by the five desires.

As we progress in spiritual studies, there comes a point when we realize that morality is not something that confines us or limits us, but that it is the only means we have to truly become free. By using morality to learn a more enlightened kind of behavior, we free ourselves from the complications that inevitably result from a life devoted to indulgence and sensual pleasure. The Buddha's teachings on morality are an inestimable gift, for they help us to discover who we really are.

Once there was a king who got lost while riding one day. As he was searching for the road back to his palace, he came upon an old house. Since the king was thirsty, he went up to the house and knocked on the door. A woman's face appeared in a window, but she did not open the door.

The king called to her saying, "Why don't you open the door?"

The woman replied, "Because I have no clothes to wear."

With that, the king took off his robe and handed it to the woman in the window. To his surprise, as soon as she touched the robe, it burst into flames. The king thought that was strange, but he didn't say anything. Instead he removed his jacket and handed that to the woman. But the same thing happened again. As soon as she touched it, it burst into flames. The king said, "What is happening? As soon as you touch my clothes, they burst into flames."

The woman said, "Last night I had a dream that you would be coming today. In my dream, I saw that I had been your queen in a former life. But during that time, I was very greedy. Whenever you wanted to donate food or clothing to the monastery, I would always complain and say that you should spend the money on me instead. That is why in this life I can't wear any clothes at all. As soon as I touch them, they turn to flames."

The king asked, "Is there something I can do to help you?"

The woman replied, "In my dream I saw that if you were to give some clothing to a saint in my name, I would be able to wear clothes again."

The king did as she asked, and only after that was the woman able to wear clothes.

Greed and immorality exact a price that we rarely see at the time. This is why this realization counsels us to be content with what we have. When we always try to get more for ourselves, we plant seeds that one day will grow into circumstances that are much more difficult for us.

The sutra says that we should "think often of a monk's garb, his bowl, and his chanting instruments." We provide ourselves with an easily remembered standard of behavior when we hold the image of a monk in our minds. By thinking often of the monastic way of life, we provide ourselves with a stable point of view from which to view life in this world. If we form the habit of often thinking like a monk, we will be much less likely to indulge in desire the next time we are tempted. With his conscience clear and his needs simple, a monk has the freedom to soar beyond this world and the troubles that are caused by living with greed, anger, or ignorance.

A monk's robe is a symbol of the material simplicity of his life. His bowl is a symbol of his well-regulated needs, and his chanting instruments are a symbol of his dedication to preaching and learning the Dharma as long as there is still breath in his body. The sutra says, "Having set our minds on monastic life, we uphold the way and purify ourselves." This line recalls the dedication of a monk and counsels us to follow his example whenever we are able. Once we have internalized this image of monastic purity and understood the fullness of it, we will be well prepared to face the temptations of the five desires, whenever they may arise. In this context, I would encourage all of my readers to seek out monastic communities whenever possible. The people living in them are not all perfect, but each of them has given his life to the well-being of sentient beings. The Buddha created a monastic institution, and he asked all of his followers to respect it and learn from it. The Buddha is the doctor, the Dharma is the medicine, and the Sangha are his nurses. You will gain much from having contact with monks and nuns, for they are the direct spiritual descendents of the Buddha's first disciples.

Even as we respect Buddhist monks and nuns, it is important to realize that not every spiritual aspirant need become one. Buddhist history is full of stories of many nonmonastics who achieved enlightenment. The important distinction to make is not whether someone has become a monk or not, but the depth of his commitment to the Dharma. While almost anyone can shave his head, only a few people can honestly give their whole minds to the truth. There are four basic ways that we can understand monastic life and the commitment it entails. In the first way, both the mind and the body are dedicated to the renunciation of worldly pleasures. When a person is dedicated in this way, he makes a very good monk. In the second way, the mind is dedicated to renunciation, but the body is not. When a person is of this type, he becomes a very good Buddhist practitioner, but he does not become a monk. In the third way, the body is dedicated to renunciation, but the mind is not. This kind of person, though he has become a monk in appearance, is not yet ready to give his whole being to his calling;

he still has many worldly desires and thoughts. In the fourth way, neither the body nor the mind is dedicated to renunciation. Though we must always try to help people of this type, it is also important to not allow ourselves to be overly influenced by their ways of thinking. People like this still believe that the deluded projections of their own harmful fixations contain all that is valuable in life. Needless to say, nothing could be farther from the truth.

If we are dedicated in our minds to the truth, it does not matter whether we become monastics or not. Emperor T'ai Tsung (627–49) of the T'ang Dynasty once said, "To renounce worldly pleasures is to become a representative of the Buddha; renunciation has little to do with outer form." It is far better to live a good life as a lay person than to live a dishonest one as a monk or nun.

Once a young woman got married and moved into the home of her husband's parents. On the third day after her wedding, she approached her mother-in-law early in the morning and asked if there were any chores for her to do that day. Her mother-in-law said there were none. "Just go do whatever you want," she said with a smile.

The young woman immediately went to a small altar in the house and knelt before it to recite her mantras. When her mother-in-law saw what she was doing she asked, "Why are you reciting mantras now?"

The young woman replied, "The most important thing in life is to understand why we are alive, so I recite these mantras whenever I get the chance."

As she turned to leave, the mother-in-law thought to herself, how can someone who is only twenty years old be so wise?

THE EIGHTH REALIZATION

The Mahayana Vow

Realize that life and death are like flickering flames, and that suffering is endless. Take the Mahayana Vow to befriend all things. Vow to take on the illimitable suffering of sentient beings, and to lead them all to ultimate bliss.

Vowing is an important part of Buddhism. The mind lies at the center of all of the Buddha's teachings. Only the mind can purify itself. The body cannot purify the mind, nor can someone else purify your mind for you. Reading can help, but reading alone cannot purify your mind. Only you can purify your thoughts and intentions. Vows strengthen the mind and harness its powers. They provide us with the impetus to keep going when we feel weak and distracted. A vow is the mind telling itself that it must become better, stronger, purer. A vow is an act of consciousness that alters the nature of the consciousness that makes it.

In a sense, we are constantly making vows. All day long we talk to ourselves and say what we plan to do. The mind communicates with itself in patterns that define who we are. If we spend a lot of time telling ourselves that we are bad, we will soon feel bad and be inattentive to the good in others. If we spend a lot of time telling ourselves that life has no meaning and that our actions do not matter, we will become careless of the well-being of both ourselves and others. These kinds of negative inner conversations can be changed. They are mental activities that can be raised to higher levels of awareness. In a very deep sense, all Buddhist practice has no other goal than to help us raise our minds to higher levels of awareness.

Vowing is an immediate and powerful way to improve ourselves. When we vow, we make a conscious change in our inner dialogue. Vows raise our awareness by changing what is happening in our minds. First we restrain ourselves by refraining from harming others, then we listen to ourselves in deep meditation, and lastly we change ourselves by consciously internalizing the wisdom of the Buddha. Vows naturally arise from a deep understanding of this process.

It is no small thing to "vow to take on the illimitable suffering of sentient beings, and to lead them all to ultimate bliss." Simply contemplating a vow of this magnitude improves us. Imagining the millions of sentient beings before us who made this vow is an experience that is as humbling as it is inspiring. Taking on the illimitable suffering of sentient beings means to suffer for them, with them, and in place of them. The purpose of doing this is "to lead them all to ultimate bliss." This is the core of Mahayana Buddhism. One stands before it in awe. This vow is a crucible that will change the world. It is the key to enlightenment. It is the absolute center of the Buddha mind. The *Flower Garland Sutra* says, "Make the great and compassionate vow to save all sentient beings, and not to leave one of them behind."

The first realization of this sutra deals with the Buddha's view of this world. The second through the seventh realizations deal with the Buddha's views on human life. This last realization is the most important one in the sutra, for in this one the Buddha provides us with his highest level of instruction. The first seven realizations of this sutra concern what might be called the Buddha's philosophy of life. This last realization concerns his answer to that philosophy. Buddhism sometimes is misinterpreted as a passive or negative religion that counsels its followers to withdraw from life. This last realization should be sufficient proof that the Buddha never intended his teachings to be understood in that way. Not only did Shakyamuni Buddha ask us to vow to take on the sufferings of others, he also showed us how to do this by the example of his own life. Following his enlightenment, the Buddha spent forty-five years teaching others how to liberate themselves from delusion. The entire second half of his life in this world was dedicated to taking on the sufferings of others.

The Buddha taught that merely understanding the abstract doctrines of no-self, emptiness, impermanence, suffering, and nirvana is not enough. Buddhism is not a religion of mere abstractions. All of the ideas discussed in this sutra are meant to be used; they are meant to be used in the task of leading all sentient beings to ultimate bliss. This task is begun by understanding the philosophical aspects of the Buddha's teachings, but it is only completed by implementing those teachings.

All Buddhas and bodhisattvas have vowed to take on the illimitable suffering of sentient beings, and to lead them all to ultimate bliss. This basic vow is known as a "general vow." The specific ways that different Buddhas enact this vow are known as their "specific vows." The vows that Buddhas make commit them to something, but they also give them a sort of power that is called the "power of the vow." This power arises from the fact that their vows create forces that are unimaginable to ordinary people. Entire Buddha realms can come into being on the strength of a single vow. A vow thus can also be called a "basic cause" of some-one becoming a Buddha. When the forces of the mind all are marshaled toward the same goal, there is nothing that can pre-vent success. The only thing that can limit the power of a con-scious vow are the unconscious forces of greed, anger, pride, doubt, and ignorance, for only these forces can cause the mind to fall back into its customary tangle of harmful fixations.

The vow to take on the illimitable suffering of sentient beings, and to lead them all to ultimate bliss is often called the "Mahayana vow." *Mahayana* means "large vehicle." Mahayana Buddhist prac-tice is centered on the good of all sentient beings; it is based on the intention to carry all of them to the shores of ultimate bliss. To practice Buddhism without making the vow to save all sentient beings is to leave out the most important part of the religion. It is like plowing a field and then forgetting to plant any seeds.

The Mahayana vow is often described as having three parts. The first part involves the awakened mind, the second involves the compassionate mind, and the third involves the methodical mind. Master T'ai Hsu said that the awakened mind is the cause of the Mahayana vow, that the compassionate mind is the basis of the vow, and the methodical mind is the completion of the vow. The methodical mind is that part of us that tries to be effective in teaching others and leading them to the truth. All sentient beings are different, so we need to learn to use many different methods for helping them.

Many years ago Shariputra, who was on the verge of becoming enlightened, made the Mahayana vow. To test his resolve, a heavenly being came down to earth and pretended to be a child. The child sat on the roadside where he knew that Shariputra would pass. As Shariputra neared, the child started crying. When Shariputra saw how sad the child was he asked him why he was crying. The child said that it was none of his business, and continued to cry.

Shariputra said, "I am a disciple of the Buddha. My deepest intent is to help others. Please tell me why you are feeling so sad."

The child said, "It's no use. There is nothing you can do to help."

Shariputra said, "Please tell me! Maybe I can help."

The child said, "My mother is ill and she is going to die. Her doctor said that the only way to save her is to make a medicine from the eye of a living saint. It is hard enough to obtain an eye from a living person. To get one from a saint is impossible!"

Shariputra said, "I will help you!"

The child said, "But how?"

Shariputra said, "I have dedicated my life to others, so in a way I could be called a saint. I am willing to do whatever I can to help others. You can have one of my eyes." With that he leaned toward the child and said, "Just pull out the one you want!"

The heavenly being who had been transformed into a child said, "Oh, I couldn't do that! I would be harming you! It would be better that you pull it out for me."

With that, Shariputra gouged out his left eye and handed it to the child, saying, "Here. This is for your mother. I hope she gets well soon."

The child looked at Shariputra and said, "Oh no! You pulled out the wrong eye! I have to have your right eye! The left eye is not good for this kind of medicine."

With that, Shariputra gouged out his right eye and handed it to the child.

The child took the eye, but then suddenly said that it smelled bad and that he didn't want it. He threw it down on the ground and stomped on it. Then he yelled at Shariputra saying, "This eye stinks! How can you expect me to give something like this to my mother?"

Shariputra eventually became enlightened, but this story is a good reminder that the path is not always an easy one. The *Flower Garland Sutra* contains a long passage explaining that sentient beings are mean, ungrateful, stupid, lazy, nasty, and rude, and that if you are really serious about saving them you must be prepared to be treated very badly. The Mahayana vow is not for weak spirits. It requires that we be ready and able to apply the Buddha's teachings to some very difficult situations. The Buddha taught that there are eighty-four thousand kinds of delusion and that we therefore need to learn many different methods for helping others. A method that works well with one person may not work well with another. When we vow to help others, we must bear in mind that the help that we provide needs to do some good. We are not being helpful when we use methods that do not succeed.

Our use of wise methods should be founded on what might be called "wise compassion." Compassion is an emotion, and it is based on our ability to empathize with others, and yet to be effective with others we must also use reason. If someone steps on a piece of glass, our emotions may tell us that it will hurt them to pull it out, but our reason will tell us that they will be hurt even more if we do not pull it out. Wise compassion means that we use both emotion and reason to understand the needs of others. If we really want to fulfill our vows, we must learn how to communicate well. First we must listen, then we must think and feel deeply, and only then we can make a good decision. Most of the time, people just need to have us listen to them. Simply listening to others opens channels of compassion and wisdom that often do more to effect changes for the better than all other methods combined.

But how are we to listen? First, we must listen to ourselves. If we know ourselves, we will be better able to understand others. There is a Chinese saying that expresses this idea quite well: "to know yourself is to know others." Master Lin Chi is famous for having taught his disciples to know themselves as "real people not limited by social interpretations." Most of Ch'an Buddhism is directed at getting people to know themselves as they really are. This is why Master Ta Chu said that "the wise seek to understand the mind, not the Buddha." This statement is neither abstract nor mystical. It is very practical. Ch'an masters make jokes, startle their disciples, and sometimes talk in riddles in order to force people to see themselves for what they are. When we know ourselves as we really are, we will be in a good position to help others. When we do not know ourselves, we labor under the forces of unconscious harmful fixations. Though we may want to help, we will likely cause more harm than good.

Do not be afraid of yourself. Learn who you are and then use your wisdom to help. No matter what you have done, your experiences can be used to help others as long as you have come to fully understand them yourself. Who better to help an alcoholic than a former alcoholic who has cured himself? Who better to help a young person with low self-esteem than someone who felt the same way at that age? There are eighty-four thousand kinds of delusion.

If you have succeeded in curing yourself of one or two of them, there will be someone who can benefit from your help.

When we help others, powerful forces always come into our lives to help us as well. While we may be making the Mahayana vow for the first time, we should not forget that there are beings all over the universe who made this same vow eons ago. When we join their ranks, we will be noticeably empowered by their strength and by their concern for us. Our lives may not seem to change all that much at first, but if we are receptive, as time goes on we will learn to sense their presence, and to call on them for help. You are not alone. When you vow to help others, you join the most benificent group of beings in the universe. Powerful forces will come to your aid because you have earned their respect, and because your intentions are directed toward goodness. When we turn away from our selfish and harmful fixations, we join with forces that are greater than anything we can imagine.

Once there was a novice monk who was walking with his master. The monk had been thinking about the Mahayana vow for days. At last he said, "Master I am ready to vow to dedicate my life to saving all sentient beings in the universe."

His master was delighted. He turned to the young monk who was walking behind him and said, "Here. Give me that heavy pack you are carrying. And please, now you must walk in front of me."

The young monk felt awkward but he did as he was told. He gave his heavy pack to his master and began strolling ahead with his arms swinging at his sides. After a few hours of this easy pace, he noticed a large ant hill on the side of the path. As he contemplated how many sentient beings there were in just that one ant hill, his resolve began to weaken. He thought to himself, "I don't think that I really do want to save all sentient beings in the universe for there are so very many of them. I should concentrate on saving myself instead."

His master, who had considerable psychic powers, heard his thoughts. The moment the young monk concluded that he would concentrate on saving only himself, he said, "Here. You can carry this heavy pack now. And it is time for you to walk behind me again."

When we are not committed to our goals, they are rarely if ever accomplished. When we are committed to our goals, powerful forces come to our aid. If our goals are wholesome and beneficial to others, there is nothing that can stop us from accomplishing them, for our resolve will draw on the greatest source of energy in the universe. There is nothing stronger than compassionate awareness, and there is nothing greater than loving kindness. As we bow humbly before these gentle forces, we will discover that we are flooded with a strength that is greater than any other in the world.

CONCLUSION

Approaching the Awakened State

These eight points are the realizations of all Buddhas and bodhisattvas. With diligence they trod the way, with compassion they hone their wisdom. They board the vessel of the Dharma body, and sail to the shore of nirvana. Then they return to the cycle of birth and death to help others cross to that shore. These eight points can direct us in all things, and they can show all sentient beings how to understand the sufferings of birth and death; they can help us disentangle ourselves from the five desires and turn our minds to the saintly way. If a disciple of the Buddha chants these eight points, thought by thought will he eradicate his infinite karmic debt; and he will approach the awakened state, and quickly become enlightened; then he will forever be free from the cycle of birth and death, and abide in joy forever.

The Dharma teaches us how to "approach the awakened state." It does not simply give us this state. The concluding section of this sutra tells us that if we practice the suggestions made in the sutra, we will "quickly become enlightened." Part of the enlightened mind is turned toward the needs of others, while part of it is turned toward the needs of the self. In the highest sense, compassion is a state that transcends the individual, and thus it is also a means for entering upon the Buddha mind.

Enlightenment arrives after years of practice. It is difficult to become enlightened because thought must be used to cleanse thought, awareness to purify awareness, the mind to control itself. It is like using a hand to grip itself, or an eye to see itself seeing.

Master Huang Po (d. 850) was once asked, "Delusion blocks our view of the true mind; how are we to remove delusion from our minds?" The master replied, "Being deluded and removing delusion are the same thing, because both of them only give rise to more delusion. In the deepest sense, delusion has no basis whatsoever. It arises out of how we think... When we succeed in being attached to neither the enlightened nor the unenlightened state, we will achieve the Buddha mind."

Master Ta Chu said that using the ordinary mind to understand the enlightened mind is like "a parrot learning to talk—it makes the right sounds, but does not know the meaning of what it says. It is like using water to wash water, or fire to burn fire."

When a disciple asked Master Huang Po which was his true mind, the Buddha mind or the ordinary mind, Huang Po said, "How many minds do you think you have?"

How many minds do we have? All of the Buddha's teachings are directed at getting us to use our minds to see the one mind that resides in all things. Buddhist masters often speak in paradoxes because the only thing that prevents us from attaining the

Buddha mind are the limitations of our minds. Enlightenment is often called "liberation" or "ultimate freedom" because it is a state that is beyond all confinement, all error, all inner blockage. The *Sutra of the Eight Realizations of Great Beings* is a short description of how to apply the teachings of the Buddha to the events of our lives. None of the techniques described in this sutra can be done for us. When the Buddha asks us to contemplate impermanence, he is asking us to understand a basic feature of our lives. When he asks us to contemplate that the five skandhas are empty, he is asking us to realize that the very foundation of our "individuality" is comprised of nothing but illusions. The deeper we allow ourselves to see this truth, the deeper will be our understanding of life, and the quicker will our enlightenment arrive. No one can see these things for us. We must do these contemplations ourselves.

Once there was a very devout Buddhist practitioner who walked to her temple every morning for services. One day, as she proceeded in the dim light of early dawn, her foot stepped on something. At the same time she heard a "croaking" noise under her shoe. Since it was still too dark to see what she had stepped on, the woman continued on her way to the temple. And yet as she walked, she felt terribly guilty for she was sure that she had just killed a small frog. Her guilt was compounded by her knowledge that the frog had been killed while she had been on her way to the temple. All during the morning service she felt sorrow for what she had done. On her way home, she examined the path with great care to see if she could find the frog and bury him properly. Then suddenly she saw the truth of what had happened—lying in the path were a couple of dry bean pods. She stepped gingerly on one of them and heard the sound that she had heard that morning. Greatly relieved, she hurried home to continue with her day's activities.

Sometimes we imagine that we have done something harmful when we have not, and sometimes we imagine that we have done something good when we have not. The teachings described in this sutra are intended to help us see beyond all delusions, all dualistic thinking, all false appearances of separation and individuality and the greed and fear that arise from these. Master Huang Po said, "If we are always thinking in terms of absolutes, then we are making a mistake. The way to end this mistake is to contemplate that all things are empty." The contemplation of emptiness helps us overcome all of the many delusions that lie among the dualities of this world. The woman who feared that she had stepped on a frog limited herself needlessly by her mistake. Fortunately, she corrected herself by going back along the path and discovering what had really happened. Her return journey was like a contemplation, for it gave her the opportunity to reexamine her assumptions in the light of truth.

Life does not always allow us to go back along its paths to find out what really happened, but it does allow us to stop and think about the way our minds work, and the ways that we choose to conduct ourselves in this world. Only the mind can overcome the mind. A Buddha is created from a human being. The way to quickly become enlightened is to apply these teachings to the events of your life.

MAKING YOUR MIND AS LARGE AS THE UNIVERSE

An Interview with Master Hsing Yun

Master Hsing Yun

MAKING YOUR MIND AS LARGE AS THE UNIVERSE

An Interview with Master Hsing Yun

by Tom Graham and Venerable Yi Jih
translated by Tom Graham

Master Hsing Yun resides in a plain middle-class house when he visits the United States. The house is near Hsi Lai Temple in Hacienda Heights, California. Master Hsing Yun founded Hsi Lai Temple in 1988. We visited him one evening in July 1999. Our talk lasted about an hour and a half.

Master Hsing Yun, who was born in 1927, entered Ch'i Hsia Shan monastery in China when he was twelve years old. He endured rigorous physical and spiritual training until he was twenty-two years old, when he was stranded in Taiwan during the communist revolution in China. His early years in Taiwan were marked by obscurity, hardship, and an undaunted independence. Since then, he has founded Fo Guang Shan, the largest Chinese Buddhist monastery in the world, and Buddha's Light International Association, the largest Chinese Buddhist organization in the world. He has over one million followers. Though the years have slowed him down somewhat, his strength and vitality are very much evident in his eyes and in his deep voice. Parts of our conversation appear below.

Master HY: …Buddhism must not be put in a cage. The form that it takes can be anything. You can never confine Buddhism to a set of rules or laws or procedures. The deep truths of Buddhism are ultimate truths, supreme truths. The forms of practice that are used in this world to express or invoke those truths can be anything at all. Anything that leads people to the truth has value. That which makes them feel afraid, or lose respect for themselves, or for others—that is not Buddhism; that is just more of the relative world of birth and death and suffering.

Shakyamuni Buddha taught the truth. He also taught that we must be willing to adapt that truth to the conditions of the societies in which we find ourselves. Buddhism in China is different from Buddhism in India or Japan. As Buddhism grows in Europe and America, it will take on new forms that express the needs of the peoples in those societies. This is good. The purpose of Buddhism is to end suffering by teaching people how to understand themselves. The form that this teaching takes is valuable only if it attracts people to the Dharma. Shakyamuni Buddha spent forty-nine years showing the world how to end suffering; he taught people how to find freedom. He did not teach them to confine themselves within the narrow limits of an intellectual cage.

TG: Master, I wonder what you think is the right kind of practice for Westerners? What should we be focusing on?

Master HY: The best single thing to focus on is the bodhisattva way. The purpose of the bodhisattva way is to aid all sentient beings in the universe. How do we aid them? Firstly, we aid them by being generous with them. Generosity cures greed. When we are generous we help ourselves overcome our own greed as we show others that there are better ways for sentient beings to interact. Generosity teaches people to expand their awareness beyond the confines of what is normally valued in this world. The bigger you make your mind, the bigger the world you live in. Being generous is the right way to begin making your mind as large as the universe. Generosity can take many forms; we can be generous with what we say, or how we say it. We can be generous with our time and our emotions. The deep purpose of generosity is to show others that we care about them. In that moment of sharing, we become a Buddha.

The second aspect of the bodhisattva way is morality. The basic meaning of morality is this—do not harm or violate other sentient beings in any way. Do not interfere with them. Do not trouble them. Do not cause them to feel fear or worry. Once you can do this, you will become very peaceful. An enormous freedom can be found by following the Buddha's basic rules of restraint. Once you have learned to restrain yourself, you will really be in a position to actively reach out and help others. If you have not learned to restrain yourself, however, you may cause harm when you think that you are bringing help.

TG: Can you give us some examples of what you mean by this?

Master HY: Whenever people try to confine or limit other people without having a good reason for doing so, they are violating them. This is especially true when force or intimidation is used. For example, in America there still are people who use force to prevent others from getting an abortion. No one should get an abortion without good reason, but the decision of whether to do so or not should be made by the people who are most closely involved. Some stranger who adamantly declares that abortion is wrong is just speaking words. He is not the one who is going to have to raise the child. The woman who is pregnant is the one who should have the most say in the matter. She should consult her conscience and decide what she thinks is right. The conscience is a magnificent guide; it will rarely lead you astray. The Buddha emphasized the importance of understanding our intentions in all that we do. When we take the time to deeply contemplate our consciences, we will almost always see what the right thing to do is. Buddhism is a religion of self-awareness. This is another reason why it is wrong to force others to do what we think is right. We should encourage others to look at themselves; that is enough.

Ven YJ: Why do people find it so hard to restrain themselves from interfering with others?

Master HY: There are many reasons for that, but the best reason can be found again in the bodhisattva way. People lack patience and tolerance. After morality, patience is the most important virtue on the bodhisattva way. Patience cures anger and aggression. Patience begins with physical patience. First we learn how to endure the hardships of the body—heat, cold, hunger, illness, and pain. Once we can do that, we can begin to learn how to be patient with others.

Patience teaches us to tolerate others and to leave them alone, to not interfere with their happiness because of some belief that we have about what is right or wrong. Morality should teach us to be restrained in our behavior; it is not a guidebook for interfering in the lives of others. People who cling to rigid moral rules are no different from people who cling to wealth or fame or sensual pleasure. Buddhism is a religion that teaches the elevation of consciousness by understanding the truth. It does not teach us to cling to a single system of understanding, or a limited set of moral injunctions.

TG: Your discussion of physical patience makes me think of people who are terminally ill and suffering from great pain. Is there ever a time when it is right for someone like that to decide to end his life?

Master HY: Yes. If one knows that nothing lies ahead but the continued physical suffering of a terminal illness, and if one has meditated on the subject for a long time, then it is not wrong to decide to end one's life before one's disease has run its full course. The heart of the matter, once again, is the conscious intention of the individual. It is his life, and he can make that decision for himself.

TG: What if the person is unconscious or unable to do anything for himself?

Master HY: Then the members of his family can make the decision for him. The important thing for them to be sure of is that their motivation springs from love. They must make their decision based on their love for the person who is dying.

TG: What if there are no family members and a doctor must make the decision?

Master HY: He also can make this decision. But he too must make his decision based on love. If his intention springs from love and if his decision has been carefully considered, it would not be wrong to end the life of a person who is suffering from an unendurable terminal illness. Now let me ask you a question: is capital punishment right or wrong?

TG: It seems wrong to me.

Master HY: Why?

TG: Because it is a form of killing.

Master HY: No. Capital punishment is not necessarily wrong. If the laws of a nation are fair and if they are justly implemented, then the death penalty is not wrong. A person who commits a capital offense in a state like that is simply reaping what he has sowed.

TG: But what about the executioner? Isn't he creating bad karma for himself?

Master HY: No. He is just enacting the laws of the state. Responsibility for what is happening lies with the person who committed the crime. This is why I say that Buddhism must not be put in a cage. The rightness or wrongness of capital punishment is up to the people of the society in question. We cannot make an absolute statement about it.

Buddhism is a very broad based religion. It really can accept anything. Do you think a Christian could be a Buddhist?

TG: I am not sure.

Master HY: Yes, definitely. A Christian can be a good Buddhist. If someone who is a Christian also wants to say that he is a Buddhist, Buddhism has no problem with that. As Buddhists we want to make our minds as large as the universe. We do not want to confine ourselves to rigid forms. I doubt that most other religions would want their followers to say that they are Buddhists, but from our point of view, it would be fine for a Buddhist to say that he is also a Christian, or a Muslim, or a Jew. We have no problem with that. We want to make everybody feel welcome. We want everyone to feel hope. If we cannot give hope, why would anyone want to be a Buddhist? If we really have the truth, why should we care about the forms that people use to study it? Our goal is to help people, not to confine them.

Ven YJ: Master, you have discussed three of the six paramitas so far—generosity, restraint, and patience. Can you tell us how the other three paramitas should be understood by Westerners?

Master HY: The other three paramitas are diligence, concentration, and wisdom. In my observation, most Western people are quite diligent. I often see Westerners sit down with a book and not get up again for hours. They are eager to learn. If they apply this same diligence to the teachings of the Buddha, they will learn quickly. Eastern people sometimes think that Westerners are slow in the way that they do things. In China, people always try to do things as quickly as they can, but this often leads them to make mistakes. The Western way is very good for Buddhist practice; if each thing is put in the right place, and understood in the right order, there will be no mistakes. The Dharma is a very high teaching, but it is also very practical. If each point is studied carefully, rapid progress can be made.

The paramita of concentration or meditation is important for settling the mind and helping it to see the original purity that already lies within it. Meditation teaches us to see the sameness and equality of all sentient beings. I think that Western people already have seen deeply into this point. The pluralism and democracy that characterizes most Western societies arises from a deep understanding of the human mind. What is needed is for people to build on these sensibilities. The Dharma includes these truths, but it also goes beyond them. The Dharma can show us how to actually experience our oneness with all life in the universe.

The paramita of wisdom is placed last on the list of the six paramitas not because it comes last, but because it is the most important of them all. All of the other paramitas can be understood in terms of wisdom, and only wisdom can teach us how to live in accordance with the other paramitas. Unwise morality confines us and limits us. Unwise generosity may bring aid to people with terrible intentions. Unwise diligence can make us harsh and unforgiving. The six paramitas are guides to the bodhisattva way. Properly used and properly understood they will show us how to become enlightened.

Western people have enormous wisdom. They have created sciences and fields of study that are now standards all over the world. And yet, they spend too much time bent on material considerations. Consciousness itself is more important than all of the matter in the universe. Spirit is a subject more worthy of investigation than any other field. I do not mean by this that everybody should just drop what they are doing and join a monastery, not at all. What I mean is that Westerners should build on what they have learned in the sciences to include the deeper truths of the Dharma. When they begin to apply supreme truths to their studies, there will be a revolution in their consciousness.

This is one of the reasons why it is important for us to direct the dissemination of Buddhism both toward ordinary people and toward scientists and philosophers. When the high culture of the West absorbs the truths of the Dharma, there will be many changes made at all levels of society.

TG: I wonder if we could ask you to return briefly to the subject of morality. Many people nowadays live together without getting married. Do you have anything to say about this?

Master HY: Marriage is an institution that reflects the values of the society that supports it. If the people of a society no longer believe that it is important to be married, then there is no reason why they cannot change the institution of marriage. Marriage is a custom. Customs can always be changed. We can find the same core point in this question as we have in others—the ultimate truth of the matter is that individuals can and should decide for themselves what is right. As long as they are not violating others or breaking the laws of the society in which they are living, then they are free to do what they believe is right. It is not for me or anyone else to tell them that they must get married if they want to live together. That is their choice and their choice alone.

The same analysis can be applied to homosexuality. People often ask me what I think about homosexuality. They wonder, is it right, is it wrong? The answer is, it is neither right nor wrong. It is just something that people do. If people are not harming each other, their private lives are their own business; we should be tolerant of them and not reject them. However, it will still take some time for the world's Buddhist community to fully accept homosexuality. All of us must learn to tolerate the behavior of others. Just as we hope to expand our minds to include all of the universe, so we should also seek to expand our minds to include all of the many forms of human behavior. Tolerance is a form of generosity and it is a form of wisdom. There is nothing anywhere in the Dharma that should ever lead anyone to become intolerant. Our goal as Buddhists is to learn to accept all kinds of people and to help all kinds of people discover the wisdom of the teachings of Shakyamuni Buddha.

* * *

Venerable Yi Jih is a nun in Master Hsing Yun's Fo Guang Shan order. Tom Graham is a translator. He lives in San Diego, California.

The "weathermark" identifies this book as a production of Weatherhill, Inc., publishers of fine books on Asia and the Pacific. Editorial supervision: Jeffrey Hunter. Book and cover design: Noble & Israel Design. Production Supervision: Bill Rose. Printing and Binding: R.R. Donnelly. The typeface used is Fairfield.

佛弟子、常於晝夜、至心誦念八大

一覺悟、世間無常。國土危脆。四大

為無主。心是惡源、形為罪藪。如是

二覺知、多欲為苦、生死疲勞、從貪

三覺知、心無厭足、惟得多求、增長

佛弟子、常於晝夜、至心誦念八大

一覺悟、世間無常。國土危脆。四大

僞無主。心是惡源、形爲罪藪。如是

二覺知、多欲爲苦、生死疲勞、從貪

三覺知、心無厭足、惟得多求、增